HAUNTED SPIRIT

FRANCES WADHAM

authorHOUSE®

AuthorHouse™
1663 Liberty Drive
Bloomington, IN 47403
www.authorhouse.com
Phone: 1-800-839-8640

Published by AuthorHouse   09/10/2012

ISBN: 978-1-4772-2687-2 (sc)
ISBN: 978-1-4772-2688-9 (e)

This Book

is dedicated to

the memory of the life of

ELIZABETH FRYE

without whom

this book would not have been written

ONE

It was the dead of night. I woke up with a start. Suddenly. Disoriented between our two worlds of sleep and wakefulness. Confused, I turned over in my bed and put my head back on my comfortable pillow. I rubbed at the back of my head and turned over in bed, closing my eyes to go back to sleep. Aah, lovely. "What had roused me?" I thought sleepily as I snuggled down again. Warm and cosy. But there was a prickling feeling at the back of my neck, irritating me, preventing me from my slumber. "What's this?" I wondered drowsily, scratching my head. A peculiar sensation. Tingling. Keeping me awake. Hairs standing up at the back of my head. It was like a cold shiver, at first, even though I was warm. "Brrhhh, someone just walked over my grave," I thought, tossing and turning over again. Then a prickling sensation was creeping slowly but very deliberately, up the back of my head, something clinging, like a giant spider, its' feet digging into the back of my head where I couldn't see it. Crawling, from the nape of my neck in a line up to the crown of my head, leaving a tingling pain where its' feet had trodden. Hurting, painful. "Something's wrong" I thought, "with me. Must be some sort of odd headache." I looked at my bedside clock. The time was

1.30am. I reached my arm out behind me to rub the back of my head to ease the pain. I turned over yet again, trying to get comfortable. I was facing towards the window. Before I could close my eyes something attracted my attention.

A curling mist was slowly seeping through my open window. It was a small window in the middle of the bay, at the top, which I always keep open for ventilation, the curtains only half-drawn to allow for the fresh air. By now I was fully awake. "What's going on?" I puzzled, sitting up in bed. The prickling at the back of my head had not abated, in fact it was getting worse, like spines or needles digging into my scalp, but my curiosity had been aroused by this strange mist. I looked beyond the window into the pale night. It was September 1999, it had been a beautiful sunny day, and the sky outside was quite clear, the stars twinkling brightly, the moon at half circle showing itself clearly.

So where was this smoky mist coming from? It was creeping through the window and swirling about in the room. I leaned forward, looked through the glass to see if there was a fire, or bonfire, that was causing it. But I could not smell any smoke, and I was tired, and the sensation of prickling at the back of my head was still irritating me, hurting. Whilst I was still contemplating the source of the peculiar mist, a crying wail exploded into the room.

"FIND ME! GIVE MY BONES A HOLY BURIAL!"

And then, dead silence. Nothing. No sound at all. I lay there, in shock. "WHAT?" I thought, "WAS THAT?" The silence was stunning in itself. The echo of the high-pitched scream seemed to have filled the room, and then to vanish. I thought I had imagined it, after all, I was extremely tired, but what with these happenings, the prickling on my head, the smoky mist, and then the loud scream, I was wide-awake. But the noise of the scream seemed far too loud to have been anything other than real. So who was shouting at this time of night outside my house in a quiet peaceful residential area? And what a peculiar and weird thing to cry out! Whilst I was debating this with myself, trying to figure out some sense to it, a woman's voice it was . . . . then it came again, a gut-wrenching, high-pitched scream . . . .

"FIND ME! GIVE MY BONES A HOLY BURIAL!"

The noise from the wail echoed around the room, almost bounced off the walls. I sat up in bed. It certainly was not coming from outside, it seemed to be inside the room. I looked around but there was no-one there, I hadn't got burglars playing sick jokes on me, or anything like that. I wasn't even frightened by it but was fascinated by the peculiarity of it. It takes a lot more than that to scare me, but I did think to myself "What on Earth . . . . or in Heaven . . . . is going on?"

This wasn't happening. What? A cry in the dark of the night? From whom? It couldn't be real. Yet I was very much awake, and if I had misheard the first plea, I certainly heard the second one. It was a woman's voice, and she sounded desperate. An incarnate voice, coming from nowhere and filling the room, but she was pleading for help, and she sounded real. Despite my disbelief, shock and discomfort, I decided to reply, and said out loud "Who are you? What do you want?" No answer came. I looked wildly around the room, my head spinning first one way then the other, and then straining my eyes to study the darker recesses. My eyes were staring, my hair literally standing on end. A shiver went down my back. My legs and feet were tingling with a freezing sensation. And all the time, pins and needles, at the back of my head, feeling as if it was in an iron grip of sharp nails, gradually constricting, getting tighter, hurting. The opaque curling mist was still swirling around inside the room, pouring in from the small open window, its' fronds dissipating into the air inside. It seemed to be hovering, waiting.

I couldn't understand what was going on, but in my overtiredness my brain associated the misty vapour with the pleading screams, as I thought, "Is this a ghost talking, *no, screaming* at me! *Pleading* with me?" For I had realised that the scream did not come from outside, it was inside the room. Not only inside the room, it was . . . . *inside* . . . . *my head! Weirder and weirder.* My weary brain took over, and instead of being frightened, I thought, "Oh, well, if it's inside my head, I'll have to think my words." So, I concentrated as strongly as I could with "Who are you? What do you want?" and I did not have to wait for an answer. Straight back it came, almost immediately, as if in a conversation, the outside thought placed inside my brain. "My name is Elizabeth Frye" the voice said, "I was hanged as a witch in 1692" in a soft warm female tone, the panic of her earlier cries gone from her speech.

My reaction to this sudden revelation was to grab my notebook and pen, which I always keep by the side of my bed, a habit of mine for many years as I find it useful for writing reminder notes for the next day's work before going to sleep. "I'm going to write this down" I thought, "or in the morning I really will think that I've dreamed it!"

Elizabeth Frye continued, her soft-toned voice warm and gentle, "There were seven of us, we all got hung and then byrned." (The spelling was written like this in my notes) "You were one of us and went by the name of Jane Meadowes. I am so glad that I have found you at last."

"What? What is this? Am I entering some kind of nightmare while I am awake?" I could not believe, understand or comprehend what I had just been told. According to this disembodied voice that had invaded my sleep and my life, I had lived before as 'Jane Meadowes', had known 'Elizabeth Frye', and both of us had been hanged as witches! Unbelievable! Whilst I was deliberating on this thing that was happening, the voice that was Elizabeth's changed once more to a desperate cry.

"MY BONES HAVEN'T BEEN BLESSED! I WANT A CHRISTIAN BURIAL!"

"Where are your bones?" I thought automatically in reply to the question, without thinking, I was so astonished. "Winchester, or London" Elizabeth faltered in reply. Was this a conversation? While this strange communication was going on, I could see images, pictures of scenes flashing before my eyes, like watching an old movie flickering with projected slides, but inside my head. Incredible! And then the scream, in desperation, came once again.

"MY SOUL TO DAMNATION UNLESS SOMEONE CAN HELP ME!"

And then the vaporous opaque mist gradually disintegrated as it disappeared through the small open window into the night. As I watched it vanish, staring open-mouthed, I realised that the pressure of the prickling sensation on the back of my head had gone, and so with it the presence of the 'person' or spirit who had been communicating with me.

The peace of the night had returned, but I could not sleep now. I was wide awake and extremely startled and worried. I looked at the window, outside the window, and saw a clear night sky. I looked at my notes and then at the clock. It was 2.30am. So this, whatever it was, had been going on for an hour. It had seemed more like two hours. Well, I certainly had not dreamed this; my notes were written in front of me so I hadn't been asleep. Were they wild imaginings? An over-active mind? But why should I wake up in the middle of the night for my brain to invent such things? I hadn't been watching any horror movies recently, so was I in fact going mad? All these thoughts and many more raced through my mind as I tried to make some sense of it all. It was so illogical, but if I could find no other explanation, then had I really been having a conversation with a woman who had died over 300 years ago? Had this really happened, that I had been woken up in the middle of the night by this woman Elizabeth Frye with her weird revelations, and desperate pleas and cries for help? This experience disturbed my mind so much that I felt exhausted by it. Talking to a ghost! How stupid! Such foolishness! Huh! I am a very practical person, and although I have a good imagination, I am not fanciful. My mind could not accept this. It must be fantasy, I thought, as I put down my notebook. I decided that I had better try to get some sleep and forget this. I had to be up early in the morning for work, it was going to be a busy day.

TWO

The following morning I woke early. I must have fallen into a deep sleep, perhaps from exhaustion after my experience, but now I awoke with a start and was immediately consumed by the memory of the night's events still vivid in my mind. Had it been a dream or a nightmare, I wondered, as I dragged myself out of bed, went to the bathroom, and then made myself a cup of tea. I felt lethargic, but after all, I felt as if I had been awake for half the night. The remembrances of the night before were embedded in my brain, soul shocking. A woman, screaming in the night? Telling me things? That I didn't want to know? Was I even interested? Or was it, after all, just a bad dream?

"Oh, my notebook!" I thought, remembering that I had written or scribbled notes in my 'dream'. I snatched up the book, to prove it wasn't true—but yes, there it was, all there, written down in my own hand. So I definitely had not dreamed it. My notes were quite legible on a new page of my notebook. This thing *had happened!* Oh, God help me. I did not understand this, this . . . . whatever was going My mind was full of this 'visitation' to the exclusion of er thoughts, and without analysing what I was doing so wrapped up in myself, I swung myself around to sit on the edge of the bed, picked up my pen and began to write a more detailed account of my night-time experience while it was still fresh in my mind. I neither knew nor questioned why I did this, it just felt right and important at the time. I had learned over the years to trust my instincts (I was 45 years old at the time) for they usually turned out to be right. When I had finished writing down the remembered details of this peculiar event I looked again through my notes and realised the absurdness of the situation. "Impossible! Ridiculous! How can this possibly have happened?" I asked myself. But I had the original notes written by my own hand in front of me, the notes that I had written in the middle of the night.

The realisation came to me that I was not going to be able to forget about this for a while; the experience seemed to have embedded itself into my brain. But I must dismiss it, I had a lot of work to do, I was thinking as I got myself ready for the day. I had no time for frivolities or fancies such as this 'dream' had caused. However, all that day I felt distracted from my job as my mind kept wandering back to the crazy happenings of the previous night. I decided that I would not, could not, discuss this with any of my colleagues or friends. My own common sense told me that they would not understand; after all I did not understand it myself. They would think I had finally flipped, or was mentally deranged, or laugh at me, or all these things.

Anyway, I convinced myself, it was a one-off: weird ar peculiar certainly, but it wouldn't happen again. Mayb was something I had eaten that didn't suit me. That r however, when I went to bed, I did feel a little une lay awake for a while, eventually drifting off to sleep. I slept well, and nothing untoward happened during the night. The next morning I felt refreshed and decided that I must dismiss the strange idea that I had talked to a ghost, that a spirit had called out to me for help in the night. I must stop thinking about this; it must have been a dream after all. "Certainly an odd dream," I mused, "but . . . . oh, stop it, forget about it. It was a dream, you dreamed it." But a nagging feeling somewhere in the back of my mind still told me that it really had happened, that what the ghost or spirit had said was, in fact, true. I had the notes, the "proof" written down, that I had written in the middle of the night when I was awake.

Forget it? I just could not get it out of my head, however hard I tried. And I did try, believe me, but my mind kept wandering back to the event, to try to justify it, or make some sense of it all. I just could not make any logical explanation for any of it, and called it a dream so that I did not have to acknowledge any other answer. Could it possibly have been a supernatural happening; or ESP? I had not invited this spirit or thing into my life or invoked it; in fact it was the complete opposite in that my mind had been invaded, and without my permission!

I am not frightened of ghosts, unlike the majority of us, which was probably a blessing in disguise. Since I was quite a small child, my belief or instinct has been that ghosts are merely people who have lived and passed over into the afterlife, now living in another form as spirit. I have encountered them before in the form of shapes or 'shades' they are referred to, passing by, that nobody else saw at the time, or seeing someone standing on the pavement, and then when I looked back, there was nothing there. Many people have seen similar things. However, I had never come across one of them talking to me, or asking—no, screaming and pleading—for help.

I remembered clearly the words of the spirit or ghost of Elizabeth Frye. She had told me that I had lived another life in another time over 300 years ago, in the name of Jane Meadowes, and that we knew each other, apparently, to our deaths! "By hanging! And then the bodies burned! Charming!" I thought sarcastically, trying to make light of it. I have an abhorrence of evil and wrongdoing, and thought to myself. "How terrible and cruel to have died like that. And if she is to be believed, then I also died like that!" The projected images of the previous night came into my mind. A cottage on a hill by the side of a dirt-track lane, a strange looking cart and horses, a long gallows with seven nooses blowing in the wind.

THREE

It was around ten days later, and although still puzzled and curious by my encounter, I had not been disturbed again and decided to put it down to an over-active imagination, or perhaps I had eaten something which disagreed with me and had caused some kind of hallucination. Whatever it had been, it was not relevant to my own busy lifestyle, and I had dismissed the event.

I had gone to bed as usual, without a single thought of my peculiar visitation, which was by now only an old memory. Around 2.30am I woke up suddenly, feeling that someone had tapped me on the shoulder. As I roused myself from sleep, I could once again feel the prickling sensation around the back of my head, but the feeling was more gentle this time instead of the burning urgency of the pins and needles which I had felt before on that other occasion which I had tried so hard to forget. I blearily glanced around the room but could see nothing except the darkness, and was relieved, thinking of the last time this had happened. I rubbed my eyes to clear my vision and looked towards the window. "Oh! No mist! Good! Now perhaps I can get back to sleep," I thought, snuggling down into my warm duvet.

"Must have been a noise in the road, or a car turning." I live in a cul-de-sac, and cars often come down the road, either by mistake or just to turn around, at all times of the day and night. I settled down, starting to feel the welcome drowsiness of sleep approaching.

Then a voice sprang into my head, shaking me out of my relaxed state, a sweet, soft gentle feminine tone, not my voice and not my thoughts. "It is Elizabeth" the voice said, "I have escaped from the devils that are chasing me. I have wanted so much to come and visit you, I hope you don't mind." There was a pleading in her soft tone of voice. I jolted awake again, thinking, "Oh no! Not again! This isn't real, it's my imagination" and tried to push away the intrusion, close my mind to it, close my eyes, shut it out whatever it was, and go back to sleep. I didn't want to know. But I could feel the presence of another person, Elizabeth, in the room. I opened my eyes yet again and checked around the room, but could see nothing except the night. As my eyes focused, I looked towards the window, and through it, and could see nothing except for a clear sky, complete with stars on a cold autumn night. What was happening to me? Where was this coming from? I had a lot of unanswered questions, both for myself and for my 'visitor', whoever or whatever she was. I had never dismissed the first visitation as pure fantasy, even though I had tried hard to convince myself. Maybe, subconsciously, I was hoping that she would come back, for it was certainly very weird and my curiosity had been aroused by the previous encounter, and had not been satisfied. Whilst I was musing on these thoughts, I noticed that my senses had been assailed by a wonderful perfume that pervaded the room, a fresh scent similar to a hazy warm summer breeze mixed with the subtle hint of sweet wild orchids, honeysuckle and roses. I was sitting up in bed, waiting, and did not feel cold at all. Then I heard her again, that soft female voice in my head, pleading with me. "Please listen. I need you to help me. I want to tell you something of my life, and of yours." Elizabeth spoke so gently and yet persistently, a quiet whispering in my head.

I felt I had to make some kind of decision. Was I going to listen? Curiosity nagged at me, although I must admit I was apprehensive. "Why pick on me?" I thought mildly to myself, knowing in my heart that I was accepting the invitation, my natural inquisitiveness overtaking any misgivings or wariness, or fear, of this very odd situation. As if in answer to my unasked question, Elizabeth replied "Because you are the only one who can help me."

"Strange reply," I thought. A little trepidation was fluttering in my heart but I wanted to hear what she had to say to me. I turned on my bedside lamp and reached for my notebook and pen, both accepting and resigning myself to this strange situation. If we were going to have another "chat" I most certainly was going to keep a record, write it down, whether this woman or ghost was a witch or not, but mainly to try to keep my sanity. "No, I am not a witch, and neither were you, we were both innocent." Elizabeth replied, once again answering an unasked question. The spirit was reading my thoughts, she was *inside my mind*, there could be no lies here, only truth. There was no hiding place for deception, just *pure bare honesty*. I knew, then, that as it was for me, so it was and could only be for Elizabeth, a two-way bare souled communication. A lot of people would probably by now have been scared out of their wits, but she (the voice) was not frightening to me. It was very strange in that it was a voice in my head without being able to see a person.

As I was trying to grasp this and come to terms with these astonishing circumstances, Elizabeth spoke again. "I wish you no harm, I love you, but I need you to help me. *Please.* I do not have long before they will come looking for me." Presumably "they" were the devils from which she said she had escaped. I acquiesced, gave in gracefully. After all, it wouldn't do any harm to listen, and afterwards I could make up my own mind (when I got it back to myself!) what I thought of it all, what conclusions I could draw, for I was still a little dubious as to whether "Elizabeth" really existed. "Oh well, I'll go along with it" I thought.

"Thank you, my dear" came the swift reply. And Elizabeth began to tell me of her life, or rather to show me her life. She did not use many words, but projected images, pictures of living moving scenes, events and happenings, into my head. It was rather like watching a movie, with a flickering similar to the first old movies when the scene changed from one event to the next. It was not in bright technicolor, but more muted colours as you would see them at dusk with the colours slightly faded. It made no difference whether my eyes were open or closed. I tried it, and the images kept coming. Even when my eyes were open I could see nothing of my bedroom, only the pictures being transported into my mind, and I could neither control nor stop them. She showed me her cottage with the thatched roof where she had lived with the surrounding woods and the dirt-track lane, which led to it, and the nearby village. Something else that I noticed was that there was no sound with the pictures, only occasional words from Elizabeth. She was relaying these pictures to me when her presence along with the marvellous perfume seemed to fade away, the communication between us became weak, and then she was gone. After she went, I felt as if I had had a real conversation with a real person. There did not seem to be anything "supernatural" or spooky about it, more like an old movie being shown to me by an old friend that I hadn't seen for many years, without the need for many words in explanation. After this visitation, I looked at the clock. She had been with me for about an hour. I lay awake for several more hours, wondering, surmising, dismissing, was it a product of my own imagination playing tricks on me or, again, did this really happen?

A few nights later, Elizabeth came again to visit me. I was by now beginning to associate the gentle prickly sensation in my head with a visitation, combined with the marvellous honeysuckle rose perfume which pervaded the room. Elizabeth gradually unfolded the story of her life and death to me, visiting once or sometimes twice a week over several weeks, usually on a Tuesday or Wednesday, and on Saturday or Sunday, and always at night between 1.30am and 3.30am. The visits lasted anytime from a few minutes up to an hour, when Elizabeth's communication would become weak and she would drift away. However, if I was tired she seemed to be able to hold away this feeling, unless it was that I was so interested that I did not notice this.

She wanted so much to tell me about her life and seemed gladdened by our communication, and sometimes relayed more than once about specific incidents that had happened which were perhaps more significant to her, giving me the stories in very graphic detail. We also had conversations, and sometimes I would tell Elizabeth about the happenings of my day. So it was not a communication with a "ghost" who was left over as a memory that only repeated an event of an accidental or violent death. This spirit had an active mind and held conversation with me, as if she was alive but without a body. She was extremely interested in my life, but did not seem to have any concept or understanding of anything to do with modern living. She simply did not understand anything to do with electricity, of telephones or faxes, TV or computers, even electric lighting. Try explaining electricity to someone who lived before it was invented! Refrigerators and freezers were not in her comprehension and were not in her vocabulary. But if I talked to her of a walk that I had taken with my dogs along a river or in the local woods, Elizabeth would ask about the various wild plants which were in flower at the time according to the season, or what the weather was like, had it been sunny or raining, warm or cold or breezy. These things, of course, make perfect sense if she lived in the seventeenth century. Although I knew that these visits were strange, I grew to accept them and became quite used to being woken at night to have a "chat" with my friendly ghost. Sometimes I wished that Elizabeth would have picked another night, as these visits usually made me tired for the next day, but I did not reject her. I did sometimes wonder why she came to talk to me because she had not told me what she wanted from me. The urgency of her initial appeals seemed to have disappeared, but at the time I did not question this.

FOUR

Over the course of a few months, Elizabeth came regularly to visit me, and recounted to me her remembrances. Some of her story she told to me in speech, but the majority was in picture form as I have described, like watching an old cine film in muted colour, flickering and faint at first, then becoming clearer and stronger. All of this happened during our night time 'chats', the information which she wanted to impart gradually given to me. Before and sometimes after each session, Elizabeth and I would talk to each other through our connection of thought processes, but all conversation stopped when she was relaying a part of her life to me. Mostly, before the end of a sequence of events, the communication became weak and she faded away, leaving me waiting for the next instalment until the next time she visited. And then, she did not necessarily start again where she had left the story on the previous occasion. Sometimes it was obvious that she had missed out a whole section of events and jumped to a later time in her storytelling. At other times she would tell again about a part of her life that she had already told to me. In talking to her before she began to recall memories, I could ask about a particular time or event, and it would depend upon how painful this particular memory was as to whether she would agree to share it. One particular memory was so painful to her that she only told me about it once, but that one time which I shall come to was recounted to me in very graphic detail. All her memories I saw through her eyes rather than as an onlooker, complete with all the emotions that she must have felt at the time. I gradually pieced together the events of her life shortly before her untimely death, and hopefully have written them in the order in which they happened. I will recount her story to you now.

A picture was placed within my mind. A winding country lane which was a dirt-track road bearing to the left out of the village, and then to the right going up a hill with the landscape rising to the right hand side, being obscured by woodland. To the left was grassland going down to the valley. A beautiful little cottage on the right-hand side, facing the lane, standing alone and about half a mile from the village, a single storey building with a loft in the roof space, of wooden construction with lath and plaster walls mixed with horsehair, wooden beams, and a thatched roof. It had a centre door with a pretty window at each side at the front, and on the side of the building as it was approached going up the hill, another window with a loft door above within the peak of the roof. It stood quite close to the lane, surrounded by grassland. Opposite were farmers' fields which ran down into a valley, and behind, around thirty yards away, was a wood which stretched up the hill. A few trees, then becoming thicker with many trees and undergrowth, wild plants and flowers, brambles, nettles, dock and lovely wild roses. A stream ran through the wood to meet the river further downstream in the valley close to the village, and was always filled with birdsong, rabbits and mice, a happy and joyous place, a home to all these creatures.

Another picture came to me of an event. It was a lovely sunny afternoon in late summer. The sun was shining; it was a warm day with a refreshing light breeze. Elizabeth and her daughter, Mary, were expecting a visitor, a friend from the village. They had all been out the day before, into the woods and hedgerows behind Elizabeth's cottage (she called it her garden) to pick wild brambleberries, filling basket after basket with the ripe fruits. Today, they were all going to make them into a delicious jam. Jane Meadowes arrived at the cottage, and went through to the living room. Houses and cottages in those days rarely had locks on their doors, and this one was no exception. Elizabeth's door was always open to anyone who called. Jane made her way up the ladder leading to the loft space to join Elizabeth and Mary, who had already started hulling the brambleberries. The room was to the right from the top of the ladder, and daylight poured in from an opening at the far end. Along the sides of the room were shelves housing lots of jars, all neatly labelled with the contents. This was Elizabeth's storage space for dried herbs, jams, and herbal remedies for various ailments. Below was a working surface, on which Elizabeth and Mary and Jane hulled the blackberries into various bowls, and below were cupboards for more storage, particularly for green herbs that would lose colour if exposed too long to the light. Together, the three hulled the ripe fruits and took them downstairs via the ladder to wash them in buckets of water that they had brought from the nearby stream. They prepared a fire with wood already gathered, and put the washed fruits into a giant cooking pot with water, ready to boil over the fire later that day and make them into jam.

Jane went to visit Elizabeth at her cottage as often as she could. She was around sixteen or seventeen years old, and although she had a loving family, helping around the house with her brothers and sisters, she was hungry for knowledge. Elizabeth was like a second mother to her, and Jane loved her very much. Elizabeth was such fun to be with, she had a wonderful sense of humour and loved life. She had a great knowledge of healing plants and herbs and would pick these at the appropriate times of the seasons, and make them into potions for healing or dry the herbs for use in cooking, and make jams from wild fruits. These she would sell to the villagers, who were regular visitors to her little cottage on the hill.

Elizabeth was also the local midwife, and could be called upon at any time of the night or day when the women of the village were in childbirth. She had helped a lot of children into the world, hence her nickname of "Old Mother Frye" even though she was only in her late thirties. Elizabeth had been teaching both Jane and her daughter Mary about the different names of plants and herbs, which were edible and which were not, and what they looked like: the uses they had for cooking, or the properties for healing various ailments. Jane was fascinated and wanted to learn.

Meanwhile, in the village, there had been a lot of talk and gossip. A group of men had arrived, and they were staying at the Inn. They were the King's Men, and Pilgrims of the Christian religion, and were travelling through the Country to seek out witches and evildoers. They were always dressed in black, with cloaks and tall black hats. They had parked a strange-looking cart with their horses at the back of the Inn, and would mingle with the villagers, listening to any gossip and asking questions, and more questions. But no-one in the village was frightened by this, these people seemed friendly enough even though they had a certain reputation, and after all, there were no witches here! The villagers' idea of a witch was someone who cast ugly spells or curses or travelled on a broomstick—anyone would recognise them a mile off by the warts on their faces or their evil ways and cackling laughter, like the crones in Shakespeare's very popular play "Macbeth". So the Pilgrims talked and asked questions, and the villagers were not afraid, they answered their probing questions and were proud of their village and its' inhabitants. They chatted readily about each other, their way of life, what everyone did for a living; the farmers, merchants, smithy, etc., and the midwife and healer, Elizabeth Frye, who lived on the hill.

The Pilgrims wrote down some of what the villagers had said, and got them to sign their names or mark the page with an "**X**" as some of them did not know how to read and write. It made them feel really important that their knowledge of their fellow-men and women and their village was so valuable to the Kings' Men and that the King and Queen took such an interest in their daily lives. The men probed them about religious matters, where they prayed, when, and how often, and attended at their Sunday Church Services. And they were all good Christians; they had nothing to fear from these religious visitors to their village.

Then, one sunny afternoon, they packed and left, taking their horses and cart with them. It was a strange cart with a wooden structure above the cart made from tree branches around all the sides and forming a roof with an opening section at the back, which had chains and a padlock to close the door. The construction enclosed the back of the cart, and made the whole look like a prison cell. It had been parked at the rear of the Inn, and on their departure the Pilgrims took it with them with their horses, and made their way up the hill away from the village. The villagers thought that they were satisfied and on their way, though the Pilgrims had already made forays to the surrounding villages during their stay without these villagers' knowledge. They had already been there, talking and chatting and asking questions.

They left the village and set off on horseback, with their peculiar cart, up the hill. As they approached Elizabeth's pretty little cottage, they slowed down and then stopped. Elizabeth, with Jane and Mary, were making blackberry jam. They had hulled most of the blackberries that they had picked and were boiling them over the fire in a huge cooking pot. They heard and saw the Pilgrims approach, the horses' hooves vibrating on the dirt-track lane with the dust rising up from behind, pulling their noisy cart. They slowed down as they came towards the cottage. Elizabeth's instinct told her there was a determined purposefulness in their actions as they slowed down on their approach up the hill. WHY were they slowing down? *And then they stopped. They had the cart. They dismounted.* They were not chatting any more, but silent. They marched towards Elizabeth's cottage with a stony stride, in a very serious manner. A dreadful premonition suddenly came upon her as she realised what their purpose could be.

Elizabeth's heart began to beat faster as she thought "NO! NO! It cannot be!" She started to panic, flitting this way and that, and suddenly cried to Jane "We must hide Mary! We must protect her!" for she knew in her heart that the men had come to arrest her and would take her child as well. She was not concerned for Jane, for she was not of family, only a visitor, and these Pilgrims would surely not be interested in her. So they hid Mary in a cupboard in the upstairs room where Elizabeth kept all her dried herbs and potions, and told her to make not a sound, and left instructions with Jane that when the men had gone, she was to take her to her own family for safekeeping and look after her until Elizabeth was freed. For although she felt certain that she herself was going to be arrested and was apprehensive, she thought she had nothing to fear—not really—after all, she was a good person who helped others.

The Pilgrims banged on the door. Elizabeth took a deep breath and calmed herself, straightened her hair and her skirts, and opened the door. Two of the men grabbed her roughly, one on either side, holding her arms. The man in charge said to her, "Elizabeth Frye, in the King's Name, you are arrested on crimes of witchery and treason against the King and against the Christian Religion."

As she protested, "But I have done nothing wrong!" they marched her to the cart and very roughly bundled her in through the doorway at the back after roping her hands together like being handcuffed. She looked towards the house at Jane with a plea in her eyes that said "Please look after Mary for me" but she said nothing out loud. The men went into the cottage, stamping their muddy boots very bold and brash. "In the King's name, who are you?" they shouted at Jane. "Why, my name is Jane Meadowes" she replied timidly. "You will come with us. Is there anyone else here?" they demanded. Jane did not answer; she was worried about Mary as she would not be able to look after her. They marched Jane out of the cottage, roped her wrists and put her into the prison cart with Elizabeth, just in time to see Mary jump from the upstairs loft and run in the direction of the woods. She had panicked when she heard the men talking to Jane, and had tried to bolt. The men saw her and ran after her and she was soon caught. Her little legs could not possibly outrun these big strong men and they picked her up by her arms, wriggling and squirming. The men did not just rope Mary's hands, they wound the rope around her, trapping her arms to her body, and tied her ankles. She was completely trussed when they threw her into the back of the cart with Elizabeth and Jane, and chained the door shut. They then collected various bottles and jars from the cottage, which they took with them. As they started to travel up the lane, the three occupants of the prison cart could see the first tendrils of smoke and then flames coming from Elizabeth's cottage as it caught fire, and was burned to the ground. The men had kicked and spread the contents of the fire over the floor and furnishings of the cottage before they left. The lovely summer's day had turned into a nightmare.

It was a very bumpy ride in the cart, for they were travelling at such speed. "Oh, my dearest Jane," Elizabeth said, "They should not have taken you as well. You were only visiting me." Jane asked "But why should they take you? You are not a witch; all you do is help people."

"I am a healer and midwife, my dear, and in these times this can arouse stupid superstitions from these very religious Christians. But I am sure there is some mistake, and when we get to wherever they are taking us, I will be able to explain matters, and I am sure they will set us free. They most certainly should let you go." Her tone was very positive and convincing, and Jane felt assured and stopped worrying.

Mary was crying. She had been very roughly handled by the men, and was now being bounced up and down from the cart, which was hitting bumps and stones in the road. She was very frightened. She had hidden herself away as her mother had told her, but when the men came upstairs she had panicked and escaped from the cupboard where she was hiding and had tried to run into the woods where she was chased down and caught. When the men went after her she tripped on some undergrowth in her desperation to get away, and she had been easily captured and thrown into the cart with her mother and her friend Jane, and did not know what was happening. She was hurt and bruised, and did not understand why they were being taken away from their home, and she was tired, why couldn't they all just go back home? Elizabeth and Jane tried to comfort her and reassure her, dried her tears and tried to protect her from the poundings of the horses and cart from the rough stony road, taking it in turns to sit her on their laps. It was a very long, uncomfortable ride in the cart. Eventually they passed through a huge stone archway, one of the entrances to the gated town of Winchester, with its' cobbled streets and stone buildings. Neither of the women knew where it was; neither had ever been very far outside of the village where they lived. The Pilgrims, their captors, pulled the horses up outside a stone building in the centre of the town.

By this time, it was late in the evening and getting dark. The building was single storey with a red and gold insignia, the King's emblem, above the centre door. It was the prison house. The Pilgrims walked around to the back of the cart, took off the chains and dragged the women by their roped hands up two steep stone steps and banged on the heavy door. They had to carry the girl Mary, as she was trussed. It was by now becoming quite dark. The door opened onto a stone flagged floor, the building lit inside by burning torches in holders along the walls. As they were escorted inside, they saw a large man in uniform sitting at a table in the middle of the room. The Pilgrims announced to this man that these people had been arrested for witchery. As the ropes were taken off them, the man sitting behind the table stood up and ordered them "You must register your names" in a hard, cold voice, "and strip off your clothes." They were terrified, wondering what was going to happen to them, horrified at the thoughts going through their minds of what the guards might do to them. But they did not dare to disobey and did as they were told, too frightened to argue or do anything else. They were helpless, there was nowhere to run, the guards were at the front door of the building to which they had been taken, and the big man behind the table seemed to be very threatening.

They all took off their clothes as they had been ordered, and stood there naked, feeling very vulnerable. The guards approached, prodded at them with their sticks. "Separate the girl!" the big man ordered the guards. Two of them stepped forward. They grabbed Mary's arms roughly, one on each side of her, lifting her feet off the floor and pulled her towards a doorway on the left-hand side of the stone walled room. That was the last time that they saw Mary.

The guard at the desk looked towards the other archway which was behind him, and pointed, ordering the other guards "Take them down to the cells." Elizabeth and Jane were prodded again with the sticks and pushed towards the stone doorway. The opening led to a twisting circular stone stairway leading downwards and very dimly lit. They were pushed down these narrow stone steps, at the bottom of which was a long corridor with an earth floor. To the left were bars going along, behind these were prison cells. The guards went along to the third cell, opened the barred door and thrust Elizabeth and Jane inside. They had been pushed so hard that they both fell to the floor. The guards locked the door and went back up the winding stone staircase.

In silence and darkness as the two women started to recover themselves, they became aware of other people in the same prison cell. Through the dimness as their eyes focused, for there was no lighting down there, they could see that five other women were huddled in a corner, all naked and very dirty. The night was growing cold and they were huddled together for warmth. They did not speak but welcomed the two women with outstretched arms to join them, and they all huddled together to keep warm for the night. And so it was that these three people, a woman, a teenager and a girl, were captured by hostile men and taken forcibly from their home in an idyllic country village. The child was separated from her mother and the other two women thrown into a dirty, dank, smelly, barred cell below the ground. They were naked, cold and very frightened, too frightened to feel hunger, or pain, or thirst, or tiredness.

FIVE

The following morning, as dawn became day, Elizabeth and Jane could see much more clearly where they had been housed. The prison cell was below ground level in a basement, with a very tall ceiling. Stone walling surrounded three sides of the square cell, with bars to the front which were bolted. At the back, almost at the ceiling, was a square hole in the stonework, which was barred with a grille, letting in a little daylight although it was very dismal. The grille must have been at ground level, for they could see boots on feet going past. Dust and dirt were occasionally kicked into the cell by the passers-by. The aperture was too high to see very much, just large enough for the light of the day to filter through. The floor of the cell was earthen and somewhat uneven. The bad odours and smell of the place was disgusting, of sewerage and rot. It made the women feel nauseated and sick. Elizabeth and Jane had hardly slept at all that night, just occasionally losing consciousness from complete exhaustion. They had talked through the events of the previous afternoon and evening, and were both extremely concerned for Mary. She was only about eleven years old and had been dragged off and separated from them.

As morning came, Elizabeth found out by talking to the other women that they had all been arrested on grounds of witchery and treason. The other women had been brought in on the previous day and had been kept in the cell, only given a little bread and water. Elizabeth asked them when they would be able to go to the toilet and to wash, as there were no facilities in the prison cell, but the other women said they had not been allowed out of the cell. Eventually they all had to take it in turns to squat in the corner when they became desperate; they did not even have any clothes or a rag with which to dry themselves. As Elizabeth told it to me, "There was nowhere to pee and it had to run down our legs."

Later that day, they heard bolts drawn back from the door leading down to the cells, and footsteps on the stone staircase. A guard appeared and offered them bread and water. Elizabeth ran to the bars of the cell and asked the guard if they could see someone in charge, to try to find out what was to happen to all of them. The guard was very aggressive, and shouted "Huh! There is no need. You are a witch, and you have been found out and captured." Her mild question seemed to agitate him. He pushed the bread and water bowl between the bars at the bottom of the cell and backed off very quickly as if he was afraid of them. "You are all dirty evil witches," he said. "You will be kept here until tomorrow, when your confessions will be heard."

"Then we are going to trial tomorrow?" Elizabeth asked, thinking that she would be able to explain, speak to someone; that somehow, somewhere, someone would listen. The guard laughed a hollow sarcastic laugh. "There will be no trial," he answered, sneering at her. "There is no need.

We have the written proof, evil witch!" He turned on his heel and disappeared back up the spiral stone staircase, and they heard the bolts thrown back into place as the heavy door slammed shut. Elizabeth had not even had a chance to ask about Mary.

The captured women all sat down on the dirty earth floor, too stunned to cry or shout their objections, the realisation coming upon each one of them that none could escape the fate that had been destined for them. If the guard was to be believed, they were not even going to be allowed a chance to defend themselves, to try to put forward their innocence. No trial! Condemned as witches! Elizabeth was so concerned and worried for her daughter Mary that her own situation seemed unreal.

For the seven women locked in the tiny cell, they were all so devastated by what the guard had said, that day seemed to be the longest day of their lives. As they sat on the bare earth floor, they exchanged the stories of their lives and found that although they lived in different villages, their lives were similar in that they were all helpers, and had knowledge of herbal potions as remedies for various ailments. Some of them were midwives and had helped the women of their village in childbirth.

As gossip spreads from village to village, they had all at some time heard that they hanged witches, didn't they? And they were all terrified. But they had a trial first, didn't they, so that they could make answer to their accusers, and there was an important person there, a Judge they called him, to decide who was telling the truth, a fair man who would listen. But this guard had said there would be no trial. He had said that they would hear confession. Perhaps that was what he meant! So Elizabeth would be able to speak, to explain the innocence of Jane Meadowes and herself. Her mind was racing, first panic, then logic, surely they would listen. She kept her thoughts to herself, and tried to reassure Jane as best she could. The Pilgrims had found the brambleberries in the large pot and had called it a witches' brew, and written it down as evidence, along with some of her jars of herbal remedies which were all labelled carefully. They had told her this on the journey. Caught in the act! But it was only jam! How could they possibly think . . . ? But they did.

The good Pilgrims who had arrested Elizabeth, Jane and Mary, had gone into the cottage and found a black concoction which had been brewing. God only knew what was in it! They were afraid to go too near to it for fear of being poisoned by the gases and steam coming from this large cauldron. They searched the cottage, and in an upstairs room found jars of dried mushrooms, poppy seeds and valerian. So their suspicions had been right, and their duty told them that they must take all three found at the cottage. Elizabeth as an evil witch, Jane as her pupil in the art of witchery, and Mary as her spawn. Who and where was the father anyway? None of the villagers knew, the Pilgrims had made their enquiries; therefore she must be a child of the devil. The child had proved this by trying to escape. Surely an innocent girl would not run from these good religious people? They had taken jars for evidence along with the statements which they had written for the villagers to sign. Some of the local people could not read, but that did not matter. The Pilgrims had a duty to rid the world of all this evil, this wickedness, and if they had to use a trick or two to carry out their purpose, then so be it. Before they left, they pulled the hot embers from the fire, scattered and kicked them around the room to make sure that the cottage and the rest of its' contents would be destroyed. Elizabeth's lovely home was razed to the ground. These heathens, all these pagans with their evil potions and wicked spells and un-Christian beliefs: the world would be a better place without them so that they could get on with the job, their main purpose, to educate everyone in the only truth, the One God. They, as Pilgrims, were ridding the world of evil. It was their duty to Almighty God. Without these dark influences and superstitions, they could teach the people without fear of prejudice. Once educated, the people would see that it was all for their own good, to save their souls. The Pilgrims believed this fervently, and substantiated the deaths of so many, mainly women, by reason of the strong convictions of their Christian religion.

SIX

Elizabeth and I had been communicating in this strange way for weeks whilst she recounted to me the story of her life and although it might seem peculiar, I was becoming quite used to being woken in the middle of the night, somewhere between 1.30am and 3.30am to be shown the next instalment, or to have a chat. It happened around twice a week, mid-week and sometime over the weekend. Sometimes when she woke me on a Wednesday night, I would get a little annoyed with her. I had to get up early for work on Thursdays at around 6am and I did not want to be disturbed to hear her stories on that particular night of the week. Throughout my doubting, this fact did make me think that she was, in fact, real, as no one except for a masochist would deliberately, even subconsciously, deprive themselves of sleep in this way. At other times, when she did not arrive and I had a good night's sleep, I would wonder where she was and felt some disappointment that she did not contact me. Although I still wondered whether she was in fact a real person or a figment of my imagination, I welcomed and accepted her as a person or spirit, separate from myself, without knowing what to believe.

I 'viewed' her memories, as I have said, in picture form accompanied by some words. It was as if I was gradually being given the whole story, and not necessarily in the order of the events as they must have happened. The memories skipped from one incident to another, very much as we recall our own memories, and with all the emotions present of love, hurt, joy, pain, betrayal, etc. The peculiar thing about her reminiscences was that *I felt these emotions* as if these events were happening *to me,* that I was seeing or re-living these events through Elizabeth's eyes and body, rather than as a detached viewer. I never saw Elizabeth in her memory pictures, as I seemed to be seeing her memories through her mind. It was both disturbing and fascinating at the same time, and I felt as if I was getting to know her as a person. I began to believe that she must be real.

Sometimes she would visit for up to an hour, then the scene would gradually fade away as she left. At other times she seemed to start to "tell" me of something but after a couple of minutes the communication would "cut off" suddenly, similar to turning off a television, and she would be gone, leaving me with the silence and darkness of the night. On a few occasions I had glimpses of her standing in my bedroom, either when she woke me or as she faded away, but as I have said, did not see her within her relayed picture stories.

The image of Elizabeth, when it came, usually only lasted a short time before she began to recount her stories, but it was so strong that I can describe her to you, along with her personality. I had the impression of a tallish woman of fairly slim build, her age being around mid-thirties. She had a thinnish long face, a straight aquiline nose, and very dark kindly yet striking eyes, which seemed to look through you to your every thought as if she could read your mind, and yet friendly and with compassion. Her hair was long and dark brown, which she wore tied neatly back into a bun at the nape of her neck, tiny curls framing her face. Her complexion was pale and her delicate features made her look quite bird-like. She was neither pretty nor beautiful, but her demeanour made her an attractive and striking woman. Her smile, which was rare, was sparkling, and lit up her eyes and her whole face. She looked to be a knowledgeable person who held a mysterious yet charming air about her, as if she knew many secrets but would never tell. She was totally trustworthy. She always wore a long dress which reached to her ankles, in a plain dark brown material gathered at the waist, with a round high neck and long sleeves, a small cream-coloured frill from a lace undergarment showing at her neck and wrists. On her feet she wore short stout boots with a slight heel.

One Sunday afternoon, I went for a walk with my two beautiful dogs along a local riverbank. It was February, it was very cold and wet underfoot, and the reeds in the river had dwindled. The undergrowth of the previous summer had faded and died down, and the narrow walkway was very muddy after the previous night's rain. A dull winter's day. My two dogs had raced on ahead of me, excited to sniff out anybody and anything that had gone before them. At the time, I had some work problems and was trying to think them through. As we wandered along the narrow walkway, a track about a foot wide, there was a willow tree along the route, the main trunk having fallen away many years before, and it had lain itself in the path of the track. In order to get by, you always had to scramble over it, but some of the branches had remained upright, or grown that way.

As I placed my hands to lean against one of the branches, I sighed with my own troubles and inadvertently said, "Oh, Elizabeth, what else can happen to me?" She had visited me on the previous night, and although I was thinking through my own problems to a logical solution, she was still in my thoughts.

I was talking to myself, but suddenly I felt that she was there with me, and she knew what I meant, knew what was in my heart. I felt a rush of warmth around me even though it was a bitterly cold and windy day, and heard her sweet voice in my head, saying, "Do not be afraid, my dear. Everything will be alright with you in the end." Well, I was stunned and shocked. The re-assurance was fantastic, but surely she did not know of the problems I was trying to resolve. I could feel her presence there and she was enjoying the natural beauty of the walk, which I was taking. It was the first time that she had been with me during the daytime, and I felt as if she was seeing the beauty of our world through *my* eyes. I could feel her with me, and she was really enjoying the walk. It seemed she was looking, seeing, through my own eyes! The realisation of this startled me and made me feel very uneasy. "Just a minute!" I thought, objecting. It was one thing 'talking' to a dead person or a ghost in the middle of the night. If she wanted to convey her memories into my mind, that was her choice, but it was entirely another matter to feel that she was with me during the daytime, inside of me, looking out!

"What is happening to me?" I thought. "Am I going completely stark raving mad? Am I insane after all? Should I commit myself to a lunatic asylum? But I am only an ordinary person," I reasoned to myself. "Why is this happening to me?" I felt as if I wasn't in control of my own thoughts, basically because they kept being interfered with, and now I was not to be in control of my body either. "Who's in charge?" I thought. I was extremely worried by this turn of events, and thought I was losing my mind, probably in need of psychiatric help. But this was not to be.

That night, Elizabeth came to visit me, woke me up again in the middle of the night, to tell me how much she had enjoyed our walk.

I was furious with her for interfering so much with my life, and I told her so. I really gave her a good telling-off, expecting her to float off and not answer me. She did nothing of the sort. She apologised profusely. She had been so enthralled by our chats about my riverside walks that she had stayed close by me so that she could perhaps get a glimpse, just for a fleeting second, of what I could see. She explained that she had missed these things so much. Then, when realising that I was so upset, she had given away her presence to try to give me some comfort, because she loved me. My anger at her use of me was now completely dissipated as I realised that she had merely been trying to help, in her own way. She promised faithfully that she would never again try to use my body or to use me in any way without my permission. I believed her at the time, and know this now to be true.

She had progressed, had gone beyond the night, and occasionally at my invitation came with me during my afternoon rambles with my dogs. Sometimes I allowed her to use my eyes, to enable her to see again the beauty of nature, particularly during the forthcoming springtime, which was a very wondrous time for her. When she saw the wood anemone, the celandines and bluebells, followed by the blossoms and leafing of the trees, she was ecstatic. Her excitement at this and the wild woodland was almost childlike enjoyment, as I talked to her along the way. I know that it lifted her heart and gave strength to her spirit, and I was glad to have a companion such as her.

I did notice that she only recognised the flowers of the wildwood and natural wild-growing herbs, but if I took her into my own garden, she did not recognise some of the cultivars of today. Sometimes when I was out walking with my dogs, I could feel her presence, could feel her burning intensity when I allowed her to look through my eyes at the beauty of everything natural; the trees, the wild roses, grasses and other wild flowers growing along the wayside as we wended our way on our walks, following a river or stream, or walking through a wood. She would point out to me the tiniest details of the flowers, with their sepals, and later in the season, the details of a mushroom or the mosses growing alongside. Sometimes I felt the inclination to lean against the corrugated bark of a very old tree, and mused that some of these very elderly trees may, in fact, have been young saplings when she was alive.

SEVEN

A few weeks after our first daytime discussion, Elizabeth came to see me at night at around 2.30am. I was awakened by a gentle touch on my shoulder, and could smell her perfume in the room. I opened my eyes to see her standing in my bedroom. She was extremely agitated, pacing back and forth, her head bowed, wringing her hands with worry and concern. "What's the matter?" I asked her. Elizabeth replied with a tremor in her voice, "I have come to tell you about the remainder of my life and of the manner of my death, my dear. I know that I have to do this. Please, will you be strong for me and let me recount this to you?"

"Yes, of course I will listen," I answered affectionately. I think, perhaps, she had come to a very important and difficult decision. She had to trust someone, which was why she had sought me out in the first place, and I believe that in accompanying me on some of my walks, she had learned to love and to trust again. She seemed to be a different person now, than the frightened apparition who had originally so dramatically burst into my sleep and my life, screaming and pleading for help months before. She had grown stronger in spirit and confidence, and some of her anger and bitterness had evaporated. Now that she was ready to face telling me about the crux of her story, I was not going to refuse her. She wanted me to know the whole truth, with nothing left out. Although I didn't know it then, this was going to be a very long night.

Elizabeth calmed herself, stopped pacing, and straightened her skirts. It was a habit of hers that I had seen before on various occasions, as if this action made her ready for 'whatever'. She placed a picture in my mind, and her memories started to spill out in scenes in front of my eyes. I could no longer see her in the bedroom; I could not even see the room any more. It was as if I was transported to a different place and time, as before in her recollections, seeing the events unfolding, vivid and clear, along with all her thoughts and emotions. Once again, I saw the memories through her eyes.

Elizabeth Frye and Jane Meadowes had been accused of witchery and treason, and captured by the Pilgrims. Elizabeth's daughter Mary had also been taken and then separated from her. Elizabeth and Jane were entombed in a prison cell below ground with five other women.

The next part of her life Elizabeth only recounted to me once. I had asked her several times about her eventual death before she was ready to recall the memories. When she finally decided that she must do this, it was in very full graphic detail. This is her story.

At dawn, the guards came down to the cells with a pail of water, and the women were told to wash. Then each was given a white smock and ordered to dress. There was no footwear for them. Once they had done as they were bidden, the guards unlocked the cell door and bound each woman's wrists, and they were marched up the narrow stone spiral staircase down which they had been pushed so roughly two days previously. There were guards both in front and behind them as they were accompanied. The women were all very frightened, their hearts racing as they wondered what was going to happen to them, holding on to a faint hope that they might yet be heard by a Judge, or have a trial, but none of them dared to ask any questions. They were taken up out of the filthy stinking cell to the square stone flagged room, which was the main entrance place of the prison. There they were made to give their names again. The guard sitting behind the table ticked each name on his list and to each he merely said "Yes." The atmosphere was stony cold. One of the women found the courage to ask, "What is . . . . (going to happen?)" and another said, "Are we . . . ." but neither got any further with their tentative feeble questions, as the guards hit them with clubbed sticks across their backs with one word. "Silence!" They all became mute from terror, and none of the women spoke again in that place.

The captives were taken outside to a waiting cart with wooden bars and wood-barred roof, similar to the one in which they had been brought to this place. The horses were already shafted and were stamping at the cobbles and snorting. A crowd was gathering as they were pushed into the back of the cart, then roped to the sides by their wrist ropes so that they were standing, facing outwards towards the crowd. The guards mounted their horses and all began to move off in convoy, some guards in front and some behind the cart. The crowd followed, throwing things and hurling abuse. "Witches!" they jeered, "Evil witches! Hang them! Kill them!" Along the route on which they were taken, others joined the crowd, all shouting and jeering and throwing stones at the captured women, who were terrified at this hostility. Some began to cry and wail. With their wrists bound to the sides of the cart, they could not escape the stones or the pain.

The convoy went along the cobbled town road and carried on down a pleasant dirt road with grass verges, some hedging, trees and fields beyond. At a crossroads, on the far left corner, the women were faced with a horrific sight. A gallows had been built, with seven ropes hanging from it, the nooses made ready. When the captives saw this monstrous construction, they all knew now for certain, even if they had not already known, that each and every one of them was going to their deaths. The horses were pulled up with the cart facing the gruesome platform. The leading horseman dismounted, and there were whisperings in the crowd. Some said he was a very important Churchman who had come to oversee the punishments. It had been a very successful foray for the Pilgrims to capture seven women at the same time so that they could rid the world of these evil crones, these spellmakers, these witches. They would make the most of this opportunity to show the people who were in charge.

The crowd pushed nearer to the now stationary cart, prodding the women through the bars with their sticks and throwing more stones, shouting cruelties at them. "Witches, dirty evil witches! Devil worshippers! Whores! Hang them! Kill them! Curse them! Let them rot in hell!" After a while, the guards pushed the crowd back and went to the back of the cart, unchained it. One by one they untied the ropes holding the women who had been forced to stand bound to the sides of the cart. Some were struggling, others still, as they were dragged onto the platform where they re-roped each separately through their bound wrists and tied them to the main gallows bar. The captives then had their ankles tied, making sure of no possible escape from their fate.

The man in charge, a High Church Official, stepped onto the platform. He was an awesome figure, dressed entirely in black, with black cloak and tall black hat. He turned to the crowd and announced, "Good people of Winchester, we are gathered here today to hear the confessions of these heathens." The crowd roared and applauded. He then called out each of the women's names and said, "You are called upon to confess your sins of witchery and treason against the King and Queen, in the name of Almighty God." As the crowd cheered, the Churchman held up his hand. There was immediate silence. A deathly silence. Even the birds stopped singing. He walked to each woman, saying as he went down the row, "Do you confess?" And each woman answered, "No, Sir, I am innocent." He turned to the crowd and said in a booming voice, "See how they lie! We have evidence and written proof against each and every one of these devil-worshippers." And to the women, "You will talk before you die. Confess your sins and renounce the devil so that you may be forgiven by Almighty God before you die. Otherwise you will rot in Hell!"

"RACK THEM!" As he shouted his instructions to the guards, they grabbed the women's legs and pulled the ankle ropes attaching them to drum-like structures with handles, then proceeded to turn these handles. The women were pulled off their feet into the air, being stretched by the ropes at their wrists and ankles. As the guards tightened the ropes, the women looked almost as if they were flying. And then—suddenly—excruciating pain for the captives as the ropes pulled taut, tighter and tighter as the guards turned the handles. "CONFESS!" the Churchman shouted above the cheers and jeers of the crowd. "CONFESS YOUR SINS!" Two of the women screamed out "I confess!" As the crowd cheered he gave instruction for them to be cut down and ordered them to stand.

"Do you confess to evil witchery?" "Yes."

"Do you renounce your heathen faith?" "Yes."

"Do you now acknowledge the One Faith, the only faith, as our Lord Almighty God, and take Him only to your bosom?" "Yes."

"Then you may die in peace." Their answers were mere whisperings; they could hardly be heard above the roar of the crowd.

He then had the guards put the nooses around their necks but made them wait for death to witness the confessions and fate of the other women. He nodded to the guards. They tightened the ropes once again, the women screaming as their arms and legs became dislocated from their joints, indescribable excruciating pain. They were kept in this disembodied state for several minutes, which must have seemed like several hours to them. Some passed out from the pain and hung there like limp rag dolls. The man of God strutted up and down the platform, inciting the crowd, his purpose clear in his mind that he would use these seven to enforce his rule, so that these ignorant people of the crowd would not dare to oppose him. He had to force them to lead a good religious Christian life to save their souls and felt it was his God-given duty to make them see this was the only true and righteous path, to rid the world of these heathen creatures. He could feel his power rising as he expanded his chest, for he was a very influential man who would not tolerate disobedience. He spoke.

"Witches! We WILL hear your confessions! In the name of the LORD!"

And to the crowd, "We do not enjoy these punishments. They are to help these women to cleanse their souls. We must pray for their confessions. It is our duty." He got down on his knees, his hands aloft in prayer, looking skywards. The gathered crowd were by now becoming quieter and a little edgy, muttering amongst themselves. They had thought the prisoners would just be hanged and that would be that, and now were becoming frightened by this awesome figure strutting on the platform and now kneeling in prayer. They no longer wanted to be there, having to watch these women in such agony. A few may even have thought, "There but for the grace of God . . ." but could not turn their eyes away.

Then, just as suddenly as he had knelt, the Churchman stood up and ordered that the prisoners be cut down. As the women fell to the platform, they were ordered to stand, but none were capable of obeying so the guards lifted their limp bodies and put their heads into the nooses. Each woman was then demanded to confess her sins of witchery. He went to each woman in turn, and three more confessed, to be spared any more tortures. By this time with the excruciating pain, the women would be glad to die, to be spared any more tortures; they no longer wanted to live in this world of pain and evil hostility from these men who called themselves righteous and good. Elizabeth, gasping for air and trying to speak through the pain, found her voice, clear and strong. "I am innocent of the crimes that you accuse me. I am a Christian. My good friend Jane Meadowes is innocent; she was only visiting me. I hope I have lived a good life and helped my fellow men and women. I am innocent and I will not die with a lie on my lips. Praise be to God."

The crowd gasped. The Church Official stamped his feet, he was getting very angry. He slapped her hard on her face, and turned to face the crowd. "You are, all of you, witness to the evil lies which come from this woman's mouth. Even now she will not renounce the devil and ask for forgiveness. Her god is the devil himself." He turned back to Elizabeth. "You are an evil witch. May you be accursed and damned to the fires of Hell." He stood in front of Jane, who could only whisper "I am innocent, I am innocent" in a pathetic little voice. He replied, "Then you, too, will be damned and burn in Hell."

He gave a command to the guards, who hoisted up the noose ropes, hauling the women into the air, and they were all hanged. The Churchman then ordered that the bodies be left hanging for ten days, as a lesson to others, before they were cut down.

The crowds dispersed, making their way back to their homes. They were very quiet now, disgusted at what they had witnessed and ashamed that they had so fervently joined in, even demanded the deaths of these women. For this man of God had left a fear in their hearts that it could just as easily have been them or one of their own in that situation, and that some or all of the prisoners may have been innocent victims of the Pilgrims.

Ten days later, the guards returned to the crossroads. They carried out their duties as quickly as they could, cut down the rotting bodies and piled them into a heap in the field. They used the wood from the gallows and collected branches from the nearby copse, making a pyre with the branches like a pyramid structure over the corpses. They set the whole on fire, which smoked and burned for days, an acrid smell blowing in the wind, until all the bodies were burnt to cinder.

EIGHT

As the scene faded away into the night, I felt mentally exhausted and physically drained. Throughout this sickening tortuous vision, every thought, every emotion; each turn of the barrels, the tautness of the rope; rope biting into flesh, excruciating pain of dislocated limbs; all the pain of the torture. I had felt it as my own pain, as if it was happening to my own body, for you see, I was re-living it in the flesh through Elizabeth's eyes. And she had to, was compelled to, recount to me the nature of her dying, of her death. And I knew that I had to bear her pain and suffering with her, had to help her through this so that she could at last face it, get through it, so that she could be released from the horror and torment that she had endured at the hands of her captors. An innocent woman had been tortured and murdered, and I could not turn my mind away. No wonder that she had asked me to "be strong".

Was this the crux of her self-imposed imprisonment of physical and mental torture, the reason why she could not go peacefully to God to be healed and comforted? Was this why she "could not see the light"? All she saw at that moment was the cruelty of the world, the injustice, and she wanted it known, wanted the wrong to be put right. It was the lies, the untruths, the injustice of it all. For she had been a good woman, a true Christian who had always helped other people and led a good life. Was this her reward? Her spirit had been broken, her faith was in tatters, and she wanted things to be put right. During her torment, the physical pain she could bear, but not the mental torture of the lies, the lies. Untrue! "Not the crowd's fault" she had thought, whilst she was wavering between unconsciousness and cruel reality, forgiving them. "They have been brainwashed, they don't even know why they are here."

Unkind! Untrue! Accused with no hearing, and no way to defend herself. No-one would listen to her truth. Lies. And they wanted her to lie before she died. No. NO. She would not lie, not to stop the agonising pain, not even if it could have saved her life. And she would not die with a lie on her lips. So she bore the pain, the excruciating pain of her tortures. But she vowed to herself that one day; oh yes, one day, she would be exonerated. One day, people would know the truth. It had to be told. She did not know how, but she would find a way.

I put my hands to my temples to try to squeeze all thoughts and pictures out of my mind. I felt that I had to get her out of my head, had to think logically. Her memories had been so horrific, and I had felt it all. The sickening dreadful pains of the torture whilst she was racked, still throbbed in my arms and legs from the inevitable dislocations of the joints, and I could still hear the tearing crunching sound of them being pulled from their sockets. The ropes biting into the flesh at the wrists and ankles was nothing compared to this. It made me feel sick to my stomach, made me want to heave. And, to be honest, I am sure that I did not feel the full impact of what she must have endured that day. How terrible, to have died like that. Even though she must have been in excruciating agony, she must have been extremely strong willed. For she did not give in, she refused to bend to the will of her tormentors to make her say things that were untrue. Her commitment to right and truth must have been overwhelmingly strong to submit to such extreme pain without capitulating. I admired her for that. I don't know whether I could have been as strong if I was placed in that situation. She should have been allowed to continue to see the beauty of the world. Why, then, even now, did I feel that I needed to prove her existence to myself? But I did.

I started to analyse the whole scene, try to make some logical sense of it all. Some of the words she used were olden language rather than the language of today, the meaning of which I did not understand. When she told me about the bodies being burned, for instance, she said, *"They were left for about ten days hanging as a lesson to others, and then the bodies were taken down and byrned on a pyre."* There was no picture with this statement, so I had asked what she meant by a 'pyre' as I did not understand the word. The picture sent into my head was of bodies piled up, with sticks arranged around them in the shape of a pyramid, tied together at the top to keep them in place. Exhausted as I was, I had to get some rest, even though I would not be able to sleep with my mind in such confusion.

The following morning, with the information I had gained overnight, I decided that I must make my own investigations in order to come to a decision regarding Elizabeth's reality, if only to prove or disprove my own sanity. I looked up the word 'pyre' in the dictionary and found her description to be correct in the finest detail. The word 'byrned' was spelt in the old-fashioned way, in Olde-English. This statement was written by me whilst I was holding my pen in my hand as Elizabeth was talking to me, as were other words placed into my conscious thought throughout our sessions. She had used strange words and olde-worlde language before in recounting her memories to me. She had told me that she died in 1692. I went to the local library and although I could find little information, I did find out that a lot of 'witches' were put to death in 1692, a fact of which I was unaware when Elizabeth told me. I had heard of the witch trials, but did not know about particular dates in history (a subject I was never very interested in at school) when they occurred, and found out that they took place mainly during the sixteenth and seventeenth centuries I also found out that at this time in history, 1692, witches in England were hanged, but in Scotland they were burned to death.

It was that one word, 'pyre' that really clinched it for me. It was not a word that I would have used, in fact I had never heard the word and did not understand its' meaning until I had looked it up in my dictionary. Therefore, logically, it had not come from my own brain. Her explanation and picture were perfect. The realisation of this now left me in an enormous quandary. All doubt had been removed, the last fragmented uncertainty erased. *Elizabeth was real.* There was no way she could possibly be a figment of my imagination. *She was a separate person than myself.* My emotions were in turmoil. On the one hand, I was very relieved that I was not, in fact, mentally disturbed and in need of psychiatric help. On the other hand, with this confirmation and knowledge, it also meant that I had another much more important decision to make.

Elizabeth had asked, no, pleaded, for help. Was I prepared to give what she had asked of me? What would this entail? It was no longer a debate of fantasy or fact. Talking to a ghost? Talking to myself? It would have been easier to slide myself onto a psychiatrist's chair, to be probed and then comforted. This was not to be. She had proved her point, my Elizabeth, with one word. Pyre. She had answered the burning question which had been eating away at my sanity. Basically, I felt that I had no choice in the matter. I could not refuse to try and help her.

I tried to recall, with the help of my notes, what she had originally told me. She had said that she was being chased by devils, and was escaping them to come to visit me. In her original pleading, she had said, "Find me! Give my bones a Holy burial!" And then, "My bones haven't been blessed—I want a Christian burial!" And lastly, "My soul to damnation unless someone can help me!"

"Well," I thought, trying to apply logic to the situation, "I haven't got any chance at all of finding her bones." According to her, they were burned to a cinder and not buried in a grave, and she did not even seem sure that Winchester was where she had been taken. Therefore she must have been speaking figuratively, and had no concept of time, for over three hundred years had passed and her bones would by now be dust. Earth to earth, ashes to ashes. Except that she had not had a funeral, had not been buried in consecrated ground nor had a blessing. She had, in fact, been cursed.

I no longer disputed that she was real. Certainly a ghost or spirit, but she was very much alive within her form. She had told me too much about things of which I, previously, had absolutely no knowledge whatsoever. The reason, she had said, that she had sought me out was that "I knew her in another life when she was alive, that I was hanged with her, that my name at that time was Jane Meadowes." Therefore, if this was true, then I had known her truly, had known her as she really was, and not the evildoer, witch, and devil-worshipper of which she was accused. Although I conceded that Elizabeth was a real spirit, I have only her word that I lived in a previous life as Jane Meadowes, and although I personally do believe in reincarnation, this is a whole issue of its' own which I do not think is relevant here.

During our communications, I had seen into her, and I believed she was a good soul. In life, she was always at hand to help, and if anyone came to her in desperation with no money to pay, she would give whatever anyone needed rather than turn them away. Elizabeth was someone you could always go to, no matter how large or small the problem, and she would help if she could. She was a person to be trusted, and never gossiped. Anyone's secrets or innermost feelings were safe with her. Tortured and tormented, she remained a good soul. When I saw into her, this is what I saw. Not a martyr, not a pariah, but a very loving vulnerable person who had been terribly, cruelly, almost irreversibly, badly hurt and caught in the crossfire of our cruel incomprehension, pomposity, and the fight for political power which at that time belonged to the Church. Protestants and Catholics had been vying for power for many years during the seventeenth century. This can also be said of many other centuries.

But how could I help her? What did she actually want from me? She had not said—not yet. I have always had a very strong belief in God even though I have never been a regular churchgoer, as I do not appreciate all their doctrines. Perhaps in this way we were of similar mind.

Prayer seemed to be the only answer. I felt I really wanted to try to help Elizabeth but also knew that I could not do this on my own. Anyway, it was not up to me, it had to be God's will. I had discussed my night visitor with my husband and my mother, who both agreed that the best course of action would be to pray for her soul to be put to rest, and also to pray for God's protection for my family and home. We sorted out an appropriate prayer from my mother's prayer book.

"Visit, we beseech thee, O Lord, our home and family and drive far from it all the snares of the enemy.
Let thy Holy Angels dwell herein to preserve us in peace and let Thy blessing be upon us evermore.
Through Jesus Christ Our Lord. Amen."

I said this prayer every night before retiring to bed, and also prayed for Elizabeth Frye's soul to be released from her torment and be put to rest. For I believe that she had great courage, the courage of her own convictions. She stood by them. And I stand by her, because I know her.

NINE

I had not seen or heard from Elizabeth for about ten days after her final revelations and was beginning to wonder where she was or what had happened to her. Was it possible that either her last confessions to me had released her soul, or that my prayers for her had been answered? But surely, if either of these was the case, would she not have found some way to come back and let me know that she was now alright, after all that she had put me through? I was not exactly worried or concerned by this; in fact I was beginning to enjoy having an excellent night's sleep every night, without disruption or disturbance. Perhaps I had driven her away with my prayers, or that God had helped her. I did wonder, and strange as it might seem, sometimes I missed her. She had not attempted to accompany me on any of my walks either, and I took my dogs out every day.

Then, one night, on a Wednesday, I woke at around 3am to the sound of a church bell ringing in single, deep, melancholy low-toned chimes, like the way the church bell tolls calling the congregation to a funeral, that deep sad monotonous single note. It seemed to come from outside, the sound seeping through my open window from a great distance away, the echo seeming to grow louder and softer as sound waves blowing in the wind. The tolling chimes became clearer, stronger, louder, as if the bell was drawing closer. And then, faintly at first, mixed with the tolling, I heard a distant cry.

"Help me! Please help me!"

The tolling bell became louder and louder as if the volume was gradually being turned up until it made my ears hurt. It seemed to be echoing around the room, almost making the walls vibrate with the . . . . **TOLL!** . . . . **TOLL!** . . . . **TOLL!** . . . . And mixed in with the ringing of the bell, the cries and pleading became louder and nearer almost in competition with the chime.

"HELP ME!" (chime!)
"PLEASE HELP ME!" (chime!)

Elizabeth's voice. Terrified. Calling me. It seemed almost as if she was screaming from beyond the grave, exploding into my head. I put my hands over my ears to try to stop the echoing noise of the bell, to shut it out, but it made no difference whatsoever to the volume of the chimes, and I could hear Elizabeth no more clearly. On and on she cried, in time with the tolling of the bell, terror in her high-pitched pleading screams.

"HELP ME!" (chime!)
"PLEASE HELP ME!" (chime!)

Elizabeth was calling and crying so frantically and piteously, as if she was being dragged away, desperate, couldn't reach me, her only contact for help. I called out to her in my mind, "Elizabeth! I am here!" but she did not or could not hear me. She carried on calling, a high-pitched frenzied wailing coming through the resounding echoes of the bell chimes.

"HELP ME!" (chime!)
"PLEASE HELP ME!" (chime!)

I looked towards the open window trying to concentrate my mind, to communicate with her, to give her reassurance that I was trying to help her, but the noise of the bell seemed to be blocking any connection and she could not hear me. The tolling bell and her pitiful cries went on for about ten minutes, and then both gradually faded away into the darkness of the night.

I felt stunned and helpless as the echoes subsided with her pleas. I turned away from the window onto my stomach, resting my head on my hands. The tolling of the bell had stopped, but Elizabeth's pleas had disappeared with the sound. Silence invaded the room as the echoing in my ears subsided, and the air seemed heavy. I was concerned for my spirit friend, wondering what was happening to her. As I started to think on this . . . . a melancholy single tolling bell? . . . . Elizabeth crying out for help, from what sounded like a great distance away . . . . why could she not reach me? . . . . was she being prevented by someone or something? . . . . I started to get really worried about her, even though I felt there was nothing I could do to help her. What could I do? She had always come to me; I had never tried to call her. I had never considered doing this, and anyway, I did not know how. Perhaps another prayer might help. As I started to think on this, I heard a very loud, hollow, mocking laugh within the room. It startled me. It sounded disembodied and maliciously evil. I turned my head from side to side, looking around the room to try to find the source of this sarcastic humour. I found it. I was suddenly focused on something happening by the open doorway of the bedroom, which was on the opposite side to the open window.

There appeared to be some greyish-white vapour spinning around in a circular shape in a clockwise direction, and although I have no explanation as to why, I was convinced that this 'thing' had somehow uttered the evil sound. As I watched—I could not tear my eyes away from it—the ball-like mass of smoky substance was growing larger as it spun around. It was turning at speed on its' own axis, in a circular motion, billowing outwards from the centre point of the mass, until it grew to about two feet round. The 'smoke' was increasing its' size from the centre, the action of spinning seeming to manufacture more of the stuff. "What the hell . . . . ?" I thought. Its' gyrating movement started to change, the spinning was still coming from the centre point of the thing, but pushing the smoke out to both sides in an upwards direction. It was re-forming its' shape; some of the vapours dropped down from the centre to form a point at the base of the thing, which was about eighteen inches from the floor. At the same time, the upward motion of the billowing smoke was growing higher on each side, until it had grown into an enormous 'V' shape. Its' height was now around five feet tall. The sides and the bottom point were now static, but the stuff was still being manufactured from the centre, and the tops of the 'V' shape were beginning to look like two gigantic arms whirling inwards on themselves. And it was still growing!

"What the bloody hell . . . ." I was thinking, all prayers for Elizabeth forgotten for now. My heart was beating faster, my chest felt as if it was about to explode. My eyes were glued to the thing. I was terrified. The prickling sensation around the back of my head had returned whilst this smoky monster was emanating in front of me, but it was a far different feeling than when Elizabeth first came to visit me. Pins and needles were stabbing in a line from the nape of my neck to the crown of my head and from this line spreading outwards like strong fingers holding my head in a vice. The pain was almost unbearable. I wanted to hold my head in my hands to try to ease the hurting and comfort myself, and to run out of the room at the same time, but this thing was in the doorway, blocking my exit. I felt rooted to the spot, I could not move, and I could not look away or close my eyes. It was as if I was being forced to watch this entity manifest itself in front of me.

I do not know how, but I knew that this monstrosity was just about to form a face. I also knew that I did not want to look upon that face, that it was entirely evil, that I dare not look upon it. But I felt immobilised, completely helpless. My mouth felt dry and dropped open in horror. Terror filled my mind. My head was stinging with pain and my legs felt like lead, useless to try and move. I felt completely trapped.

I was trying to fight against all these feelings. Suddenly, I found some courage, I don't know where from, and first anger and then faith took over. I concentrated my mind, and ordered it "By the Lord Jesus Christ, BUGGER OFF!" I felt the thought projected and flash out of my head aimed towards this monstrosity that was trying to invade my life. It was probably not a very godly thing to think or say, but I meant it in no uncertain terms. I was not going to be terrorised by some smoky vaporous apparition with no substance, trying to attack me in my own bedroom. NO WAY! My temper and determination was amazing even to me. It kept its shape, but shot up through the ceiling of my bedroom at great speed and disappeared, almost with a silent *WHOOSH!*

The apparition was gone. It would be nice to think that I had frightened it. Anyway, thank you God. Although I did not sleep again that night, I was left in peace to my prayers.

This experience left me feeling drained and exhausted but very relieved that 'it' had gone. I hoped fervently that it would not try to come back. I was also extremely worried. Elizabeth had been pleading for help, but I think it was me that was now in need of help. Through my tiredness and trying to ignore the fright that I had been given, I tried to be sensible and analyse the situation in practical terms. What, precisely, had actually happened? Bells chiming. A wailing cry for help. A manifestation. Pain in my head. But was it *all* in my head? Doubt, once again, began to creep into my mind. I pushed it away because I knew that Elizabeth was a real spirit. Had this happened because I had agreed to help her? Had her demons sent something to frighten me? If so, it had definitely worked, but not in the way it may have been intended. They did not know me, and it had the opposite effect. I have an extremely stubborn nature, very strong convictions about right and wrong, and a very strong faith in God.

Elizabeth had tried to call for help. She obviously could not reach me, therefore she must have been prevented by the "demons" that she said were chasing her. Perhaps she had been captured, and when she tried to come to me, the devils had followed her and found me. She had spoken of this previously, it is why she sometimes broke off our communication so abruptly, so that they either did not know about me, or would not be able to find me. So—if this was true—they had found me. But I had God on my side. With His help, by the good Lord Jesus Christ, I had banished the thing! I had beaten it once, sent it away, and if I could do it once, I could do it again. This strengthened my resolve more than ever to help Elizabeth out of her torment. *She had been trapped for over three hundred years! That is more than four average lifetimes!* Had she been re-living her death all this time, or wandering around in nothingness? She certainly seemed to have no concept of time. Had she been chased and trapped before, and perhaps escaped? These things I did not know. But I had asked her a question during our conversations. I asked, "Why do you always visit me at night?" And her reply was, "Because I cannot see the light." Strange.

TEN

I had made a solemn promise to try to help this lost soul Elizabeth Frye. She had told me that she had escaped from the devils and was trying to find the light to go to God. I prayed for her every night through Jesus to help her on her way and find the light. I also prayed fervently for any evil to be taken out of the house, and for Dear Sweet Lord Jesus Christ to protect my family and me. I was concerned for Elizabeth, as I had not heard from her since her desperate appeals for help, and the unwelcome apparition.

I even began to question myself as to whether I had made the right decision since this event. I did not want to put my family or myself in any danger from this pleading for help from the spirit world. On the other hand, I did not see how something like this that was surreal to them could possibly affect them in any way. They were not in direct contact with the dead. Both my husband and my mother were extremely sympathetic towards me, and very supportive, but I suppose the whole situation would seem rather far-fetched if you were not personally involved. Neither of them had experienced at first hand the meetings, conversations, or the visual memories with Elizabeth, and they probably thought that I was going a bit 'dotty'. However, they would always listen when I wanted to talk of this; perhaps they thought that if I talked it out, as with a lot of problems, it would be resolved or go away. Thinking back, they may have thought that I was going a little mental, but they never suggested this and always said that they believed me. Whether they actually believed in Elizabeth or whether they just believed that I thought her to be real, I did not ask. I could not talk to anyone else about it, friends or other relatives, so I thank them for listening. Even with their support, I was beginning to find the whole thing a heavy burden. Why me?

It was about ten days after the visit by the malicious entity. I woke up at 3am. I was suddenly fully awake. Something was happening. No noise had wakened me as far as I knew. In fact the night was very still with no apparent wind as I looked through the window at the night sky. The clouds were not moving, although there was a little chill in the air. Through my small bedroom window a greyish wispy smoke was seeping. As it came into the room, it seemed to curl away from itself and then rejoin into the substance, as if there was a breeze coming from somewhere. As more vapours poured through the small aperture, the smoky mass gradually grew larger in size, balling and billowing around itself, and drifted down silently into an oval bulky shape in front of my dressing table, which was in the bay window. Within a short time, it had grown to around four feet high and two feet wide, and was hovering about a foot from the floor of the room.

I was lying down on my back in bed, watching it. Stabbing pains suddenly attacked the back of my head, almost made me cry out. My eyes filled up with tears, mostly from the hurting but also from anger, as the crawling painful sensation crept around the back of my head and neck once again. It was horrendous; it felt as if my hair was being ripped out by the roots by some unseen hand. The barrier of pain blocked all positive thoughts to try to do something about it. I brushed the tears away with the back of my hand. For a few seconds I could not see, and I wanted to know what was going on. After all, it was *my* bedroom, and an unwelcome visitor was invading it. "Here we go again," I thought apathetically through the pains in my head, "What's going on now?"

I refused myself the automatic reaction to sit up in bed, so that I would not acknowledge the intrusion as real. I was angry, and the anger was helping me to think again. I kept my position, lying down on my back in bed, but was watching the thing very closely. "If I put the light on," I thought, "it will still be there, only then I might not be able to see it so well." To do this would also mean turning away from the grey mass, and it was still growing. It was being fed from more of the smoky curling mist coming through the little open window. "I should have shut that window", I thought, but it was already too late to do anything about it.

The smoky oval shape was growing darker and denser, and then . . . . *WHAM!* My body felt as heavy as lead, and it felt as if a two-ton elephant was lying on top of me, pinning me down. All I could move was my head and my eyes. I used them. I looked, but could see nothing over me except for my duvet. I was completely immobilised as if strapped to the bed, flat on my back. With the enormous pressure of weight on top of me, it almost felt as if I was being pushed through the bed. I tried to move my arms, then my legs, or turn over, but there was no reaction from my body, hard though I concentrated. I could do nothing except watch, a prisoner of my own body and mind. The heavy weight on my body seemed tremendous, as if gravity had altered.

I waited, completely terror-stricken. There was nothing I could do. I was forced into submission by some invisible force, and compelled to watch against my will. I was too much in awe to close my eyes, try to shut out the intrusion. The grey oblong shaped smoky vapour deepened in colour to a darker shade, becoming thicker in density, until it was nearly black. It started to alter in shape, the misty stuff looking more and more like a smoking bonfire without any flames, and still it was fed by what looked like a floating vaporous umbilical cord coming through the window, connecting it to its' invisible origin. Wisps of paler vapour began to spin away from the main bulk of the thing, forming shapes of their own behind the main mass, each one of them whirling around within its' own axis, circular balls of whitish grey gradually falling into ovals, until there appeared to be four of them: one black, and three paler versions of whitish grey behind it. As I watched, my mouth open, my heart beating at a terrific rate, the smoky shapes began to change, to alter. "The other thing changed shape", I thought hopelessly. My mind felt as if it had been frozen, with no ability to interfere or to stop the course of events. I was their imprisoned audience, immobilised and helpless.

Each of the apparitions gradually re-formed. The black one appeared to be the ringleader of the performance, followed closely behind by the others. It gradually changed shape by creating other whorls within its' mass, until eventually the entity was in the form of a figure wearing a floor length cloak with a deep hood, so densely encased that it was impossible to see beyond the garments. The whole was blacker than the night. The three behind it manifested themselves into similar cowl-hooded figures with full-length cloaks, all of the much paler grey of their smoky forms. Wisps of misty vapour still whirled around them all as the forms stabilised their shapes and solidified in substance. The umbilical cord of smoke had disappeared from the open window. Through my fear, still pinned down on the bed by the invisible weight, I think I was beginning to go a little insane from fright and my hopeless position. There was an unnatural silence in the room. No sound at all. It all seemed so unreal that I started to laugh. Silently, to myself, I laughed hysterically as I thought, "Oh! There are still some wisps left over. I wonder if there was too much of the stuff?" but I did not utter a sound. They say mad people laugh a lot.

Into the silence, a voice unexpectedly emanated from the darkest form. Surprisingly, it was a very sweet female voice, rather than a deep evil echo. It sounded very much like Elizabeth's voice as it said, "Thank you for trying to help me." There was no expression, no emotion, no intonation of friendliness or love that I had come to know in the tone of her voice. It was just a dull monotone. There was no perfume in the room, just these four ghoulish cloaked things facing towards me. My senses were aroused, screaming at me, warning me, despite the grabbing hurting pains of the pins and needles, shooting through the back of my head. I was not laughing now. Still immobile, unable to move at all, pinned down on the bed, I started to panic. There was some sort of emanation coming from these 'beings', which I can only describe as *pure evil*. It made my skin crawl. I didn't know what to do, I was trapped, but my brain was starting to recover slightly from the shocks I was receiving. However, I had not recovered sufficiently to think properly, to send a prayer or try to banish the things. I do not know how or why I said this, but I managed to answer in a small voice. "Is that you, my dear?"

They did not reply, at least not in words. As one, the black form, and the three standing behind it, each lifted a skeletal hand from beneath its' cloak and threw back its' deep hood to reveal a skull head, with hollow orbs instead of eyes. Their skeleton jaws wagged up and down, their teeth gleaming fluorescent in the moonlight as they laughed, an evil cackling sound. They were laughing at me, knowing they had entrapped me. Then their bony hands came out from their capes again, and they threw back their garmented disguises to reveal full skeletons under their cloaks. All of their bones were bright and glisteningly white as if some kind of phosphorescence emanated from them. Ribs, scapula, pelvis, leg and arm bones, all joined together by their spines, all white as polished ivory. They gleamed out from their dark cloaks as if they had been hiding a dark secret, now suddenly revealed in the luminous moonlight. Their brightness blinded my sight and I tried to look away. They were still laughing that hollow sound, it was echoing around the room and bouncing back off the walls and ceiling, getting louder and louder until it filled the room. Round and around it went, until it almost deafened me. It was *evil. The most evil cackling laughter I have ever heard.* It made my blood run cold with fear as I was forced to watch and listen to such mockery.

I wished it was a nightmare. I could wake up from that. But I was very much awake. How could I stop it and escape these mocking demons? It was a living nightmare, scrambling my brain with confusion and fright. My mind and my body were immobilised and I could not think clearly through the terrible noisy cackling. How could I get rid of these disembodied ghouls?

Despite the terror of my situation, I tried to ignore the abominable sight of the skeletal figures as they started to move towards me, their evil utterances echoing back from the walls and ceiling. I tried to concentrate my mind, to block them out. Tried to deny them, refuse to acknowledge their presence. The effort was enormous; the thoughts in my head for sending prayers had not even reached my conscious mind, when . . . . the scene changed.

Suddenly, I was plummeted downwards into what appeared to be a dark tunnel. The invisible weight on top of me had finally won, and gravity took over. My bedroom and the evil creatures had disappeared from view, and my senses now told me I was plunging down, down, down. It felt as if I had been pushed over the edge of a wide abyss, all the time getting narrower. My body was being tossed and turned around, my arms and legs flailing to try to stop it, to try to reach a wall, a side of it to cling to, falling, falling. Faster and faster, being sucked down by tremendous gravity. At tremendous speed. And the darkness, oh, it was very dark. Vertigo and a sickness in my stomach made me want to heave. I was spinning around in the darkness, head first, turning around, legs first, curling myself into a ball: where was I headed? There was complete blackness both above and below. It felt as if I was in a vortex, being sucked down by some gruesome inexplicable gravitational force. So, I was lost. The blackness encased me like a tomb. I may even have lost consciousness for a little while. Then, a little light started to penetrate through the *sides* of the tunnel as it narrowed even further, and as the gravitational pull started to ease off, my downward flight gradually became slower. This was even weirder, slowing down in the middle of a fall. As the tunnel constricted, I automatically began to grab at the sides again, to try to stop the descent, even though I knew it would be one hell of a long way to get back up again. But although the tunnel was now much narrower, and I could see vaguely in the dimness, the sides had become slimy, soft and slippery, rather than the hard rock surfaces that I had bounced off and bruised myself against at the beginning of my fall. Or was I pushed? I tried to hold on to the sides, to take advantage of the fact that I was dropping down more slowly, but the sliminess of the walls would not allow any purchase. I even tried to wedge myself with my legs against one side and my back to the other, but to no avail. Each time I tried to grab at the sides, my hands simply slipped away. The walls of the tunnel stretched as if they were elasticised, and then they started to bulge inwards towards me. Shapes of hands and of heads appeared to be trying to enter the walls from the other side, forming fists on arms, outstretched hands, outlines of heads with slimy faces like viscous gargoyles trying to break through the skin of the slimy tunnel, trying to touch me and grab at me, whilst the walls themselves seemed to be oozing with sticky liquid. It made the ugly monstrosities of heads look as if they were dribbling slime. After I saw these, I did not try to cling to the tunnel sides again.

I started to fall faster again, and the slimy walls disappeared, giving way to more of a mud-like structure, gradually widening again in the long downward passage. Atmospherics took over, and it was hard to breathe, as if there was very little oxygen. It felt very claustrophobic, as lightning followed by thunder filled the cavity. Flashes and loud bangs and rumblings filled the atmosphere as I was falling, falling. A tornado wind suddenly took over, spinning me round again and again as the speed and velocity of my fall increased to a tremendous rate. It felt as if I was being swallowed up into the bowels of the earth. The vicious wind swept me down, tossing and turning me, and sucked me into the black hole. Pure unadulterated terror was my only thought as I was hurled into this bottomless pit.

Suddenly it ended, and there was no tunnel. I don't remember hitting the bottom. Perhaps I lost consciousness momentarily. Thinking back to the speed at which I had been travelling only a few moments ago, if I had hit anything like solid ground, the force of the impact would surely have smashed my body to pieces. The velocity should have destroyed me, and yet here I was, sitting down, straddle legged, in a field. It was dusk, and the colours were muted, greyish. I looked around, my hands stretching out on the cool grass. "Lovely grass," I thought, "albeit a little on the damp side." I must have been in shock. I was certainly very groggy as I tried to concentrate on where I was. I peered through the dimness, and could make out some bushes and hedges; the whole place looked sort of wild and unkempt. There were no barriers or fences, the whole place just looked overgrown and derelict. Brambles sprang from underneath the occasional tree.

Where was I? Was I dead or alive? I did not know. I didn't know anything any more after my very long and frightening downward journey through the tunnel. The terrors of that experience will never leave me. I looked around again, trying to concentrate. It was difficult with the light being so dim, diffused. Was it dusk, or the middle of the night? Where had I landed? Was I at the end of the earth? Or in some other place altogether? The air was still; there was no wind or breeze. I was so exhausted after the performances of the evil apparitions, followed by the hectic tumbling and falling at speeds of such a phenomenal rate. I was so tired. This place seemed so quiet and peaceful. All I wanted to do was to lie back on the cool grass, put my head down and go to sleep. Lovely, comfortable grass. My nerves felt raw to the edges. I needed to relax, to regain my composure. Then perhaps I could figure out where this was, what it was all about, how to get back to my own world and my own life. Sleep beckoned me, like a drug. But . . . . and there's always a but . . . . I had to make sure that I was safe. So I resisted the overwhelming temptation to lie back, and sleep, and let any other event overtake me. I had to be aware, and I had a warning feeling as my senses started to tingle, that it was not safe here.

I had to be on my guard, I could not afford to relax or go to sleep here. Had I been sent to this place by those evil beings, pushed down that horrendous tunnel, or had I escaped from them? Had I been forced down the abyss to this dark place or had they tried to prevent me from coming here, wherever it was, by trying to grab at me from the other side of the tunnel? None of it made any sense at all. I forced myself to remain in an upright sitting position, rather than lying down. For the moment, I did not have the energy to stand up. I peered into the dimness, and as my eyes gradually became more accustomed to the dusky atmosphere, I became aware of some movement. I was not alone. The greyness of the night had hidden them. As I stared, I made out the outlines of furred creatures. I concentrated harder and identified them as cats. There were about a dozen of them in the field. They were all wandering about separately in the field, sniffing the grass. They appeared not to have noticed me, and I wanted it to stay that way. I kept still and quiet, so as not to attract their attention. They looked as if they were following various scents, picking up their paws and carefully putting them down again as cats do when the ground is damp, their noses to the grass. I watched them in silence for a few minutes as they wandered this way and that, and wondered what they were looking for. There were all sorts, and even in the half-light I could make out their shapes and colourings. Some were short—haired and a few had longer fur. The colours, although muted, were quite clear and very varied. Some were tabby, or all black, ginger, black and white, smoky grey, tabby and white, I could describe each one. They all looked like moggies or feral cats. I like cats. I have had them as pets and never been afraid of them. But these cats gave me a creepy feeling as I watched them, wondering if perhaps they were looking for mice as they sniffed the ground.

Suddenly, they all stopped their sniffing, and looked up. Stared towards me. They all turned towards me, facing me, as one, as if they had all become aware of me at the same time. They sensed my presence, and reacted as if I was an intruder, some type of threat to them. They focused their baleful bright green and yellow eyes on me, shining out of the darkness. At least a dozen pairs of eyes, all with malignant stares. They seemed to light me up like a beacon. I was now the complete focus of their attention. They stared perniciously. They looked angry. Their space had been invaded. All of them arched their backs, their fur sticking out in defence or attack, and made them all look twice their size. Their tails went up in the air, swinging slowly from side to side. They started to advance towards me. They bared their teeth and hissed, the sound echoing through the silence and the stillness. Their eyes looked huge as they glinted at me through the darkness. As they advanced, step by careful step, I knew that they were getting ready to attack me. They did not glance at each other but kept their eyes focused on their prey. They did not need to; they all seemed to know where each other was, as they gradually but deliberately tightened into a semi-circle around me. Nearer and nearer. They showed their fangs and hissed at me. I was still sitting down on the grass, my legs splayed in front of me, my hands leaning back on my arms to keep myself upright, I felt so exhausted. These creatures were trying to terrorise me.

"But . . . . they are only cats," I thought, "and I like cats." Totally illogical thought, but logic was in my head. My understanding of cats was that they were lone creatures. They did not hunt in packs. It didn't make any sense. But, none of the whole of the night's events made any sense anyway, and I was once again in danger. These cats were different. They were not normal cats. They hissed again, showing their bright fangs, their green and yellow eyes becoming like slits in their faces, full of hatred. By now they were only about three feet away from me, and I realised that they meant business. They were going to tear me apart. Some of them were ready to pounce, and I could see their claws showing as they protracted them. They were vicious and wild and out for my blood. They hissed again, getting ready to spring at me. They had not cornered me, as I had not moved since my landing in the field, but I was not capable of moving anyway. Fear was taking over my brain. They had me in their sights, and I could not take my eyes off the devil cats with their gleaming fangs and long claws. There was no doubt about it. The cats were going to tear me to pieces.

Panic was not an option. "Fear is negative, forget it," I thought, as some of them crouched ready to attack. My mind and my body started to scream. "Dear God, what can I do?" As I asked the question, in my heart I knew the answer. I had previously asked for help, but not particularly for myself. Certainly I had asked for help for Elizabeth, and for protection for my family, but not for myself in particular. Now, it was me who needed help, and quickly. I asked, for myself. "Dear God, what can I do? Please help me God." This screaming plea for help came from the bottom of my heart and soul. I did not utter a sound out loud.

From the depths of the bowels of the earth, or wherever I was, I must have been heard. I was shown the way. My mind cleared of all panic, and I felt perfectly safe as I concentrated my mind. It wasn't me that thought of it, I was absolutely too tired to invent a scenario such as this. The snarling vicious creatures were all around me now. I closed my eyes to shut them out, expecting to be torn to pieces, but I had been given an idea. I concentrated my inner mind after my desperate prayer. Nothing happened. Absolutely nothing. I was not attacked. After a few seconds, I dared to open my eyes again. My prayer had been answered, and the idea had worked. I looked around the field to see . . . . the demonic cats appeared to have changed and become harmless rabbits, and they were now hopping about in the field and eating as much grass as they could find! And, they had no interest in me; they did not even appear to be aware of my presence! Relief and thankfulness overcame me.

OK, so I was stuck in a field, but I had a feeling now that it would be safe. The field was the same, and so was the dusk, but there was no evil. The rabbits were lovely. I sat and watched them for a while. I could see their bobbing tails in the half-light. They were really enjoying themselves, with such rich grass and pasture. I laughed with relief, knowing that my desperate prayer had been answered. In the background of my mind, I could also feel anger. A terrible anger, atmospheric, coming from outside the surroundings that I could see, as if I was in a heavenly pocket surrounded by unknown evil, and yet protected from it. It was wonderful, for a haven seemed to have been created within my surroundings. What worried me was that I did not know how long this was going to last. The rabbits in the field stopped feeding. They had had their fill of grass, and feeling so safe, began to play, racing around each other, some even playing at mock boxing matches, their forepaws raised in the air, rearing on their hind legs. Spring was in the air for them.

I laughed again as I watched their antics. They were so happy, frolicking around. My laughter seemed to dissipate the feeling of anger coming from outside, it seemed to be destroying it, so I laughed some more as I looked towards the happy rabbits at their play.

I felt so good in myself, because I knew without one shadow of a doubt that with, and only with, God's help, I had defeated and overpowered the demons and the evil with love. I know, in my heart, that I could not have done this alone. I needed the help of God and had called for it when I was desperate, and I had been answered. And I do believe that whichever God you believe in, if you are as desperate as I was, and you cry out for your God to help you, he will be there for you, as mine was for me at that time. It depends, of course, what you ask for. All I know is that my prayers at that time were answered.

I was sitting on the grass watching the rabbits playing. I felt very drowsy and very happy with a feeling of great contentment within my heart despite all the horrors I had endured that night. I closed my eyes, at last, feeling comfortable enough to be safe. After what could only have been a few seconds, I opened my eyes again. I was no longer in the field; I was back in my bedroom. How I was transported there, I will never know. "I have most definitely been looked after," I thought as I felt the cosiness of my lovely, lovely bed. I looked around the room, and there were no evil entities, no smoky atmosphere, a clear view through my window. There was no weight on top of me, I was quite relaxed. Everything seemed normal; all the evil had gone. The room was peaceful. Thank you, God.

ELEVEN

I sighed with relief as I snuggled down into my comfortable bed in the familiar surroundings of my bedroom, in which the atmosphere now felt quite safe. My prayers had been answered and my God had protected me and shown me the way back from that pit of obscurity. Thank you, God, for rescuing me. I had no other answer for my questions as my mind traced back the events that had overtaken me. The murderous cats in the field, the horrors of the terrifying fall into the abyss, the abominable devils that had invaded the room and had tried to send me on a collision course to hell. All gone. Peace. *No, bliss.* Perhaps now I could get some rest. I breathed deeply and stretched my arms and legs out in my bed with the pleasure of being able to move normally, enjoying the simple freedom of something that we all usually take for granted. No weights holding me down. Happy, thankful contentment. *Wonderful.* Feeling that I was now quite safe, I completely relaxed and realised how exhausted I really was. "I must sleep," I thought drowsily, "and then perhaps I can make some kind of sense of it all."

As my mind slowly wandered, I came upon the realisation that I was, after all, not alone. "Oh, no, no, I'm too tired"

I thought. "I can't take any more, GO AWAY." She was not only with me in the room, my dear friend Elizabeth, she seemed to be hiding there. I could feel her presence and I could smell her wonderful perfume. Ashes of roses, honeysuckle and sweet wild orchid were all around me in every breath I took. Her aura was wrapped around me, sweet, kind and loving. Elizabeth. I could not see her in the room, she was merely there. But where? On most previous occasions I saw her standing in my room and could see her quite clearly. Then I understood. She had become terrified both for herself and for me, and was clinging to me so tightly that her spirit had entered my body. I don't know where, on my long journey, I found her, or she found me, but she was hiding *within me*. She had been trying to conceal herself and was trembling, too frightened to speak. I could feel her fear. I breathed in deeply, slow relaxing breaths, drinking in her perfume, to keep myself calm and then to comfort Elizabeth, mentally cradling her as you would a child. I sent out thought waves of calm and reassurance to her, with warmth and affection. As her panic abated she relaxed and I felt the anxiety slowly leaving her, though she was still clinging to me. I slowly but gently persuaded her to leave her hiding place. I felt I had to separate her from inside me, she couldn't hide there. Her image gradually appeared in the room, sitting on the side of my bed, holding my hand. She was safe—for now, but I could not protect her forever. It had taken all my energy in spiritual faith and mental strength to fight off these demons, and I was beginning to despair whether I could find the strength again if it was needed.

Upon this realisation, I experienced such a warmth of God's pure love enveloping me like a blanket being wrapped around me, safe and secure and very much loved. It is the most wonderful feeling, almost indescribable, like being wrapped around in a cloud of warm cotton wool, warm and comfortable, a heady feeling of being safe, of pure, *pure love* surrounding me. A *wonderful, ecstatic sensation. To be loved like that! And I know that He loves us all.*

God had saved me. After all the horrors, my exhaustion, finding Elizabeth again, I felt ecstatic and full of energy. This experience of God's pure love, welcoming and warm, overwhelmed me. I felt energised as if I had had my batteries recharged or replaced with new ones. I felt so full of life, it was unnatural. I know that this feeling was not my own, nor did it come from Elizabeth. This feeling could only have come from one source, from God, and he had come to help. Thank you!! Thoughts were running wildly around in my head, and I knew that there was something very special that I was being asked to do. The energy had been supplied for this very task. I was not commanded but felt impelled to try. I knew it in my heart, and felt that my soul had been touched by this warm compassion, by this marvellous love.

He wanted me to help to release Elizabeth's soul into His care and protection. God wanted her to go to Him, and would give me guidance. After all, through Him, I had rescued her and prepared her for this moment, and she could not stay in hiding with me. He wanted to comfort and look after her, and would release me from my burden so that I could live the rest of my life in a natural way. All these things I understood, as if I had suddenly been given a whole lot of knowledge all in one go. Like swallowing a book, and understanding all of the contents. Knowledge is a powerful tool. But I still thought, puzzling over it, probably from the shock of all this newness, this knowing, "How can I possibly do this? I am not a vicar or priest or holy person, I have absolutely no experience in anything like this. What am I expected to do?"

The guidance was there, and to my utter surprise, I did know. It was as if it had been imported into my brain. Now, I have never attended regular church services since I was a young child. I have never been present at a séance, or attended a spiritual church. Nothing like that. But, I have always had a very strong belief and faith in God, and do believe that you can find your God on a riverside walk, or on a hill, or in your own garden, anywhere where nature exists, or in watching the magical flight of a bird, as ever you can by dressing up in posh clothes with a pretty hat and going into a church or 'holy' building. That has always been my belief.

And now, I was being asked. I had to trust. Completely. In God. It was wonderful. A marvellous love surrounded both me and Elizabeth; it was all around us, enveloping us in a cocoon of warmth. We looked at each other and both felt the love and confidence around us, a very positive aura. I had promised with all my heart and faith to help her if I could, and now was my chance. I didn't know what to do, so I prayed. I prayed for help, from Jesus and from God, for strength to find the right path for her, so that Elizabeth could find her way. As I prayed, I found myself looking upwards towards the ceiling of my room. Through the dusky night before the dawn, a pinpoint of light appeared, glimmering like a far-away star. It seemed to come from beyond the ceiling of the room, as if we were open to the sky, out of the darkness of the night, very slowly becoming brighter, like a beam of light. I concentrated my mind on it as it gradually became larger and broader, and as it grew in size, was coming towards me. It was a beautiful light, and seemed to grow more and more definitive as I encouraged it towards us with the love that had been given to me. It descended upon and all around us, enveloping both Elizabeth and myself as if we had been picked out by some enormous spotlight.

I was not afraid, and nor was Elizabeth. The light was entrancing, spectacular. It was a part of the knowledge that I had been given, to expect this perfect light. We were surrounded by it, and could not see beyond it. The light was warm, like the sun, but not burning, and came from above, not directly, but at a slight angle. I looked, no, *stared,* upwards into the light. At its' epicentre it was so golden white and bright, but it was such a gentle light that it did not hurt my eyes. I was not blinded by it as you would be if you stared at the sun for a few seconds. This light was *different.* It was suffused with emotions of love and safety, a beautiful golden white light, with no wind or breeze, warm but not burning, welcoming with a mellow light of warmth and love cascading down, obliterating everything and every thought from view. I felt as if I wanted to float up into it, to be enveloped by it. I think that I was hypnotised, it seemed to be calling to me. But I knew that this light was not for me, it was for Elizabeth. I also knew that I had invoked it.

The tunnel of light. *The tunnel of light! This must be it!* The beautiful pure light, which Elizabeth had been seeking, was here for her. The welcoming feeling of warmth, love, and safety was overwhelming, so inviting, oh so difficult to draw my eyes away from the epicentre.

I felt light-headed as I forced my eyes away from the apex of the light to look at Elizabeth. We were now standing together, facing each other, holding hands, she gripping mine very tightly. "Elizabeth," I said, "this is the light that you have been seeking, this is the right way for you to go." We looked upwards together, standing in the glowing warmth of the light, and it felt as if we were in a timeless void with no gravity, in a vacuum, weightless and motionless, floating. I looked down and realised that we were in fact floating slowly upwards and that our feet were no longer touching the ground, we were both hovering, gradually and very slowly being drawn up into the wonderful ambience of the light. A wonderful feeling of security surrounded me as we drifted onwards. A love and loveliness such as I have never known. I looked downwards for a few seconds to see how far we had floated . . . . and had a shock.

I could see my bedroom below, and my bed, and I could see *myself,* lying on my back in bed with my eyes closed, seemingly asleep and perfectly still. I was so relaxed and had this fantastic feeling of love surrounding me, but what was I doing? If my normal senses had prevailed, I would have panicked, but I didn't feel like that. I could see myself asleep and was not at all worried by this, if anything, I felt excited. I had put my trust and faith in God and, I thought vaguely, "I must be having what they call an out-of-body experience." It was really weird, but I felt no anxiety. I did have a wish to return to my own body, to make me whole, yet I seemed to be in body form where I was, floating. I was 'out on a limb', in limbo. I had heard of people having these experiences, but . . . . I felt detached, somehow. I felt safe, but not whole. So why did I feel so good in myself, why did I not feel frightened? I felt protected.

I was standing in the tunnel of light with Elizabeth, slowly but surely floating upwards. She was clinging to me, her hands holding mine very tightly. The warmth of emotions of the light was drawing us up into itself as we travelled together, floating yet ascending helplessly and hopefully. This light was extremely inviting, warm, full of love, compelling us onwards. As we went further, Elizabeth was not as reassured as I was, and began to lose her confidence. I tried to console her but she was becoming frightened and agitated. "What is this path?" she cried. "Where are we going?" She thought she had found somewhere safe to hide with me, and had realised that somewhere along this path she would have to leave me. I knew that I had to stay calm so that I could help her, and the ambience of the light helped me to do this despite my own predicament. I encouraged her on, saying, "This light will draw you up towards peace, forgiveness, and Heaven, if you will let it." How I knew this, I don't know, it must have been within the knowledge that I had been given. "I am trying to show you a better place," I said. "There will be people there who have been waiting for you, and they will love you and look after you in this safe haven." She accepted my words, which came from my heart, and being reassured, we went further on our journey together. With gravity reversed in this wonderful light we gradually ascended, Elizabeth clutching my hands. Looking back, I think it was probably the will to want to continue that made the journey possible. I wanted so much for her to be safe, and I believe she wanted peace and forgiveness. So, together, we went on, both looking upwards towards the apex, the crux of the source of the light.

As we ascended at the beginning of our long journey, there was nothing to see except for the glowing brightness. Now, as we progressed I could see that towards the apex there were people, loving beings, sending thoughts of pure love and warmth and safety. They appeared to be waiting for us, stretching out their arms and holding out their hands in welcoming gestures. They called out Elizabeth's name in soft-toned voices, warm and encouraging. They did not call to me. I was fascinated by these people who were standing at the apex of the light. The figures seemed almost opaque, not solid, dressed in long flowing robes, some with sashes at the waist, all radiating a golden glow of light which came from within them, separate from the bright glowing tunnel of light that we were ascending.

Behind and beyond these people, there appeared to be a beautiful garden. The entrance was a low wicket gate, with hedges on either side, partially obscuring my view. The wicket gate was ajar, and beyond this were other people in the garden. It was a marvellous natural landscape, a rise going towards a perfect grassy knoll. In the valley beneath the hill, a stream gently meandered its' way through, the gentle splash of the water droplets causing mini-rainbows as they caught the light. The plants in the garden were in full bloom, the flowers causing a profusion of colour, with butterflies dancing on their petals. White fluffy clouds gently dawdled across the bluest sky I have ever seen on a beautiful hazy summer day. The vivid colours of everything in that garden, particularly the special green-ness of the grass, I will never forget. The whole place was alive with birdsong, the songs of which I have never heard before or since. The beauty of this place was absolute perfection. It was full of pure love.

What a fantastic place! Everything had a natural balance, it was so alive, each living plant or creature a purpose. The whole of nature seemed to be there in balance and living in harmony. I cannot explain how I know this, it was just a feeling that came to me while I was in the tunnel of light. Enlightenment? A total understanding of the balance of nature, of life itself, became knowledge to me then, in a fleeting moment. I knew it then, in that blink of an eye, but I cannot explain it to you now. The whole of God's Creation was there, laid out in front of me in perfect harmony, the human spirits aglow with radiating their own light, nurturing and tending everything in the garden. The Garden of Eden? Was that what I had glimpsed?

I tore my eyes away from this wonderful scene and looked towards Elizabeth. The spirits were calling her by name, lovingly encouraging her to continue her journey towards them, welcoming her. It all felt very ethereal to me, unreal, as I returned my gaze upwards.

Although the spirits were calling to Elizabeth, they were not calling me. They were holding out the palms of their hands to me, to stop me from continuing the journey any further with her, their faces worried, some saying "NO! It is not your time, you must go back!" I knew this already in my heart, was certain that my number wasn't being called. I had only been allowed this far to help and encourage, and I still had a lot of living to do on our beautiful Earth before my time was up. I felt that I had done what had been asked of me, and the responsibility had been taken over. I was free to go back to my life. After all, I still have things to do.

I looked into Elizabeth's eyes, and she looked deeply into mine, lovingly. Both of us were so excited by the magnificence of the experience, and we both felt compelled to turn our gazes again towards the beautiful spirits who were calling Elizabeth to themselves. I turned once more to Elizabeth, encouraging her to go on, and released her hands, telling her I could not go with her. As our hands parted, she seemed to panic slightly, but I reassured her again as she floated on upwards towards the spirits calling her, but looking down towards me. After we separated, I left her to continue her journey, sending my love along after her. The slight gravitational pull which we had been experiencing then ceased to affect me, and reversed itself on me as gradually I lost sight of the spirit forms, and floated all the way down into my body. As I sighed with relief, I felt at the same time totally exhausted and yet totally exhilarated. I slept soundly for many hours.

On waking, my first thoughts were of Elizabeth. I felt so relaxed and happy in the knowledge that she had found the light, the right path she had been seeking for so many years, for over three hundred years. I also felt very relieved in the knowledge that the burden and responsibility for Elizabeth's soul was now placed in safe hands.

How had I found the light for her? I did not know; all I knew was that my prayers that night had come from deep within my very soul, and from love, and they had been answered. What a wonderful, out-of-this-world, euphoric experience I had just witnessed. A rare gift of insight indeed. Literally, I felt I had been truly honoured to have been given a fleeting glimpse, if only in the blink of an eyelid, a mere twinkling of sight into the next world and what may lie beyond.

For Elizabeth, it would be a new beginning, the start of a new and happy journey into the great beyond of which we know nothing. And I thought to myself, "Look after her, please, because she really is so vulnerable and so special."

For myself, I am no longer afraid of death. Well, maybe just a little, if it is painful, but I know that will not last for long. When my turn comes, when I am called, I will go willingly and with a joy in my heart, even though it will mean leaving our beautiful world. But I know I have been sent here for a purpose, as we all are, and as I am still here I have not yet achieved my purpose or finished my time, otherwise I would not have been sent back. I still have things to do, people to see, places to go, maybe even lessons to learn, but I will enjoy every minute of it!

TWELVE

By the following night I was completely exhausted and overtired from my night-time experiences. Although by now I had utter and complete faith in God, I was very worried. I had helped Elizabeth to find the light. Would her devils now try to come after me again, try to torture me with their nightmares and dark places because they had finally lost the battle? I felt drained mentally, very weak and in need of a good night's sleep.

I made my way upstairs to my bedroom and sent up some prayers, this time for myself, and got into bed. As I pulled the duvet over myself, an idea sprang into my head. I was extremely tired, and thought to myself, "Oh, no, not again! Go away, leave me alone." This idea did not come from my own brain; I was too tired for that, neither was it frightening. It just seemed weird, but then, what was this compared to the extreme experiences I had been through? "Pure or Holy Water; put it at the open entrances to the house. It will protect you." was the idea, which had been placed in my mind. I don't know where it came from but at the time it seemed like good advice. As I dragged myself out of bed, I thought, "Yes, just one problem—*I* haven't GOT any Holy

Water." Considering this, and please remember I was very overtired, I thought of the next best thing, and boiled some kettles of water to make it as pure as possible. Filling cups and bowls, I placed them by the open windows. It was the middle of May, and warm, so I did not want to close the upstairs windows, I needed the ventilation and fresh air. It probably seems a peculiar way to secure a house, but this is what I did and afterwards went back to bed feeling relaxed, and surprisingly slept well for the rest of the night.

As the water seemed to work well, I refreshed the cups and bowls every day thereafter for quite a considerable time, also making sure that the crosses were in place. I sent prayers every night, asking God to keep me and my family safe, and after nearly a week of relaxation and sleeping normally was feeling quite well recovered. The best news was that I was not bothered by any demons of any sort; in fact I don't think I even had any dreams at all, certainly none that I can remember.

I was very happy for Elizabeth in my belief that she had gone to the light, and was now safe with spirit people who would look after her, heal her and love her. She had been so terrified and lost for so long, for over three hundred years, it had weakened her will and traumatised her fragile spirit. Even though I had myself been subjected to the evil entities which had been pursuing her, I did not for a single moment have any regrets in helping her out of the dark place into which she had fallen or been trapped. I was glad to have been able to show her love and compassion again.

One week later, I was again disturbed in the night. It was around 3.00am in the morning. I did not want to wake up but felt as if someone had roused me, gently touched me on the shoulder. I could smell that beautiful perfume in the room, that scent which I recognised so well. As I forced myself to open my eyes, saying, "Elizabeth, is this you?" I saw her standing there in my bedroom, by the side of my bed, her head slightly bowed with unhappiness. "Yes" was her small reply. I sat up.

"What are you doing here?" I asked as my mind started to race. I was really surprised. I could feel the sadness within her, and wondered for a fleeting moment if the tunnel of light had not led her to safety. After all, it had been my prayers, I who had called on God to take her spirit and save her. And she was still here with me. Was it a delusion? Had she been refused? But . . . . *no!* I knew with all the love in my heart that He would not refuse her. I had seen into Elizabeth's heart and knew her to be a sweet, kind, gentle, good soul. I would not have endangered myself for any other. "I thought you had gone to God." I said.

Elizabeth looked sadly at me. "I am going but I don't want to leave you. I love you, and I want to be with you." Her plea was simple, like a lost child.

I was worried now. If she would not go, had refused to go, she could still be in danger, wandering about. What could I say to persuade her? I could see her quite clearly, standing there in my bedroom, her head bowed, and her face full of sorrow. I could feel the hot tears running down both our faces at the thought of our separation, because, you see, I loved her too. But because of that love, our special bond, I had to convince her, had to make her see that it was the right path, the only really safe place for her. How could I do this, what could I say to make her understand?

"Elizabeth, you have to go to be healed. You are hurting so much. Jesus and God will look after you and heal you, and then you can come back to me. You have to go to the tunnel of light. Go up the tunnel and they will look after you."

She stood there weeping. "I don't want to lose you. You have helped me so much and I love you and want to look after you."

I said, "You *must* go to be healed. *You have gone half way up and come down again!*"

Elizabeth and I, she standing, me sitting on the bed, both looking, *no, staring* at each other for a long time, each to consign to our memories every detail of the other's face and spirit, our inner minds locking together in our silent communication.

Whilst we were like this, together, the grey haziness of the night was gradually changing within the room, lightening, until there was a golden aura surrounding us, and Elizabeth's form started to change, becoming opaque, a phosphorescent glow surrounding her. She was being called from beyond, herself. I could hear sweet voices, encouraging murmurings, could sense feelings of warmth and love descending upon us, although I could not understand the language of the words being spoken. But I knew that Elizabeth understood, I could see it in her expression, and this time there could be no refusal, the invitation was too strong and powerful for that.

Eventually Elizabeth spoke. "I will go—as long as I can see you again."

"Of course you will," I replied. "Go and get healed and then I am sure you will be able to come and help me. Now GO—up that tunnel of light—there are people waiting for you there. They will love you and look after you and make you better and strong, and then you will be able to visit and make me strong."

Elizabeth said simply, "Thank you. I will go now."

The phosphorescence surrounding her became brighter until it became quite golden white and Elizabeth's form became less solid, becoming translucent and opaque as she gradually blended with the light. And then it began to fade, and she faded with it, as if she had become a part of it, fused with the light, until I could no longer see either her or the light, and the room seemed to become darker than the black of night as if the light had been turned off. She had disappeared in front of me, taken by the light of God. As my eyes adjusted to the darkness of the room, I could see that the night was normal once more. The dawn was beginning to break; it was 4.30am in the morning at the start of a beautiful early summer's day. As I heard the first small 'peeps' of the birds rousing from their sleep, I put my head down on my pillow—and wept. After a little while I finally slept.

THIRTEEN

The following morning I woke with a heavy heart, and soon the tears were flowing down my face. "Why am I feeling like this?" I asked myself. "I should be happy for her." For this time I knew she had gone on her journey. There was an emptiness inside me and I realised that my tears were of grief, that I was grieving for a loved one as if she had just died. I tried to shake off this feeling, reasoning with myself that she had actually died over three hundred years ago, but that didn't work. Over the nine or so months that she was with me, I had known her so well, had seen into her very soul, and although my first encounters with her had frightened and alarmed me, I had grown to love Elizabeth very much, as one would love a sister.

For the following three weeks I felt this sadness upon me, along with a kind of loneliness, that terrible emptiness, from which the bereaved suffer. I recognised the symptoms from the loss, several years ago, of someone close to me. I did not understand why I was feeling this way and tried to ignore it; after all, I was surrounded in my life with love from my husband and family.

And then, after three weeks, Elizabeth returned to me briefly. It was at 4.00am on the morning of Wednesday, 19th June 2000. I was suddenly awake, with a feeling that I had been touched gently on my shoulder. I opened my eyes to be greeted with a great feeling of love surrounding me as if I had been given a loving hug. I sat up in bed, my knees almost underneath my chin, looking around the room, but could see nothing except the night. I whispered in my mind, "Elizabeth, is that you?" I was very excited as I waited for the inevitable answer.

"Yes" came the hushed reply. "I miss you, I love you," she said, "I wanted you to come with me."

"I know," I answered. "I love you too, but I couldn't come with you. I have my life to live here before I can join you. You can come and visit me when you can."

"Oh, I can do that—I am in you," Elizabeth said.
"What do you mean?" I asked, puzzled by her remark.
"I left a little part of me in you when I transformed to God. I hope you don't mind."

"Of course not", I replied. "Are you happy?"
"Yes", she answered. The communication was weak, and before I could ask her to explain what she had said, or anything else, she faded away into the night.

After this communication, all the grief and negative emotions that I had been feeling were washed away completely. I no longer felt sadness and was very happy for her. And I felt strangely energised, as if I had been given a boost of enormous energy.

She returned again to visit me in the early hours at 3.30am on Thursday 28th June 2000, waking me in a similar manner. She told me that she was extremely happy and was learning a lot, but was missing me. During our chat, I asked her, "Why did you ask me for help? I know nothing."

Her answer was very profound. She said, "I needed the help of a good soul, someone who had known me when I was alive, a strong spirit, to be able to pass through to God."

Elizabeth also said to me, "We have a connection that no-one can break. When you helped me to God, you let me use you and I will be eternally grateful for that. You are such a strong person in spirit and in mind: although I took something from you at the time, I left something of me in you to help you." She did not explain these statements, but my belief is that she took faith to help her and left me with her love.

Elizabeth also asked me to do something, which she truly believes will protect me, my family, and my home from evil. She sent a picture into my mind of an embroidery which she wanted me to make, and to frame it and hang it in my home. Whilst she was talking to me, I drew the picture. Afterwards, I thought, "I haven't done any embroidery since I was about ten years old, and that was only chain-stitch flowers on a traycloth! How does she expect me to make this?" I asked my mother, who had a booklet of embroidery stitches which she lent to me. I found some hessian, and drew the pattern on it in pencil, and learned how to do the stitches required to make the design that Elizabeth wanted. I found an old picture frame that my grandfather had made (he was a carpenter) and have re-varnished it. It took me a long time, but the embroidery is now complete, and duly framed, and it hangs on the wall above my bed to protect me, as she desired.

For we have a bond that death cannot break—

Our love for each other

She has taken faith, love and strength from me

And left her love and strength—her gift—within me

and

ONLY LOVE MAY ENTER

a*nd*

GOD IS LOVE

ABOUT THE AUTHOR

The author has had the ability to 'see' ghosts all her life. This is neither curse nor blessing, just plain fact. She is not a medium who contacts the dead. Born in West Midlands, United Kingdom. A lover of nature and animals, Frances lives happily with her family and dogs.